FORGIVING FERNS

Books by Don Egan:

Spiritual Detox

Life: What's That About?

What Is Your Problem?

Searching for God

Rhythm of Life

There Is No Shortage!

Grief Encounter

Stranger in the Mirror

A Word About Your Healing

That's the Spirit!

available from
www.rsvptrust.co.uk

FORGIVING FERNS

**The fascinating true story of
forgiveness and restoration
against all the odds**

the story of

Noel Pattern
as told to
Don Egan

ISBN 978-0-9561209-0-8

Published by
Ferns Emerald Publications
Suffolk, United Kingdom

In memory of
Niamh Nugent, née Kilty
(1974 – 2006)

This is the true story of my life.
However, the names of some people and
places have been changed or omitted to protect
the identities of individuals.

Contents

I dedicate this book to my wife, Claire, who has remained steadfast, sincere and true in her love for me and has been alongside me for over a decade.

A wonderful companion, friend, soul mate, best friend and a brilliant parent to our two children, Stephanie and Kimberley.

Foreword

I count it a great honour to be asked to contribute these few words at the opening of Noel's book *Forgiving Ferns*. In some small measure it enables me to meet you, his reader, but in far greater measure I am humbled and honoured to have played a part (however small) in his story. This is a book I am sure you will never forget and if you get to meet Noel, he will be a man you will never forget either!

I first met Noel in 1996 at one of my earliest London 'Psalm Drummer' meetings and he has only ever been an inspiration. He is a passionate Irishman, full of poems, jokes, songs and the love of drumming. He is an encourager, a generous and courageous man with a smile. Noel always adds to the occasion, he is always willing to help and whatever is going on, he is making new friends and cheering the troops along. As you talk with him, he will surprise you with his depth of insight and is just as likely to leave you holding your sides in laughter. Noel is a true joy-bringer and great fun to be around. I have definitely been changed in meeting him and remain glad we were brought together through

'Psalm Drummers.'

Over the years of his involvement Noel has developed as a player to become a faithful host of regional 'Psalm Drummer' meetings. He has also helped in the organisation of many of our wider national events including 'Heart to Drum 07', when we gathered 550 drummers together for worship in the UK. He has joined me as a team drummer on many occasions, most notably, playing for The Archbishop of York and at principal prayer events including ceremonies at St Paul's Cathedral, 'The Call' at Reading's Madejski Stadium 2004 and 'Calling all Nations' in Berlin's Olympic Stadium in 2006. Noel has also travelled twice with me to India, where we have shared together in the work of supporting, teaching and praying for some the world's poorest people.

It was several years after meeting Noel that I became aware that there was more to Noel's life than meets the eye. I certainly had no idea of the extraordinary story this book contains. In many ways why would I know? He hadn't told me. But is that enough? Why do we assume to have any idea of the journey travelled by those we meet? It is clear we can be so self-focused that we march through life indoctrinated by our own experiences and perceptions. I can certainly confess to that. But, at the same time, the signs are there and most who have experienced hardship wear the journey of those experiences on their faces.

Watching the struggles of the world pass before us is the norm today. It should, in theory, give us greater insight into the true needs of others. However, television news reports, documentaries, film and TV drama feed us such an intense cocktail of human experiences that we are left numbed. The media feeds us a diet of extreme experiences which daily jump from severe suffering to euphoric romance. To process truth becomes close to impossible. Discernment is crushed and bows to pragmatic thought. Instead of being more sensitive, we have become apathetic to the genuine experiences of others. So much so that we fail to read the faces of those enduring struggles nearest to us. These are the ones we can help.

Noel's story is one of those and despite the extraordinary events these pages contain, he is not unusual in having been let down by those nearest to him. There are people near you today who carry the unresolved traumas of rejection, abandonment and abuse. I hope that as you read this book, a level of discernment will be restored to you, too, to sense the hidden pain of those near us.

I believe this hope remains the greatest wonder of Noel's story and as you read it, you will discover a man who is no longer the product of his background. Noel is more than a conqueror. He is a man who has discovered the only true pathway to success. Noel knows the one guaranteed and applicable method for leaving the destruction of the past behind, whilst still retaining and celebrating the blessings of his heritage. Noel has found the love and grace of God as found in Jesus.

Without this and the love and support of those around him, and without forgiveness, meeting Noel would be another story altogether!

"And forgive us our sins, just as we have forgiven those who have sinned against us." (Matthew 6:12)

Terl Bryant, founder and director of 'Psalm Drummers' and author of *A Heart to Drum* and *Rhythms of Fire*.

Introduction

I first met Noel Pattern in Ipswich, a few years ago, seemingly by chance. He'd read a couple of my books and said he needed my help. He told me he had a story that he wanted to tell but didn't know how to go about it. We met several times, usually in Starbucks, as his story unfolded. Eventually I agreed to help him write this story.

As I have pieced together the story from Noel's notes, his stories over coffee and various newspaper articles, I have been on a journey myself. It has taken much longer than I anticipated. At times I felt I had been to the dark place where Noel has been. Sometimes, in the early chapters, I wept as I typed. I thought of so many other stories like this one that will never be told.

I have worked carefully with Noel to give the reader an indication of the horror of what happened, whilst keeping the darker scenes brief in order that the reader may not give up and miss the later miracles of the story.

I have tried to keep close to what Noel told me, whilst giving some background information for those who have never been to the Republic of Ireland.

Noel is a 'big, ginger, Irish fella' who loves to drum. That he is still alive is a miracle. My hope is that, as you read his story, you will realise that however bad things may get, there is always hope. This is Noel's story and it has been a privilege to have a small part in bringing it to a wider audience.

Don Egan

August 2008

Chapter 1

The Beat of Another Drum

It's difficult to explain to an outsider. There was a deep thrill in the heart of this 6-year-old boy, as I stood in Gorey Main Street, with my two brothers, David and Pat, and watched the St Patrick's Day parade. Coming from a long line of Irish bagpipers and dancers, I stood by the roadside in the crowd. I was excited by the sound of the pipers. The militant snare of those drums stirred something in my soul as I watched the parade that day. The strident beat of the drums demanded my attention. In many ways, this sound reflected the rhythm of life in this southeast corner of the Republic of Ireland. We were 60 per cent unemployed, 85 per cent Catholic and a 100 per cent Irish.

Childhood, back then in Ireland, was so different from today. Children were told to do things and not do things – "Do this. Don't do that." We received instruction from a hierarchy of adults and we were to obey without question. We were not to think for ourselves. We were to obey. Resistance was futile. It would be met with a beating.

We had to obey our parents, our teachers and the priest. We had to march to the beat of their drum or be beaten ourselves. The cane and 'the leather' were feared by every Irish child.

Corporal punishment was later outlawed, after I transferred to the technical college at the age of 16. But even then, teachers and Christian Brothers were not afraid to launch a wooden chalk duster across the room, aimed at any disruptive boy, clocking him on the head and covering him in white chalk dust.

The deeply-engrained Catholic culture meant that we were not to think for ourselves. We were to obey the instructions of adults and especially the priest, who was viewed by all Catholics as the 'Pope of the parish'. Everyone looked up to him. Our religion was our culture.

My two older brothers and I had to be in church on Sundays and we were in real trouble with our parents if we didn't know which priest had said Mass. The first question when I got home from supposedly going to Mass was from my Mum. She would always ask, "Who said Mass?" I would always know because I would pop into the service just to see who was saying Mass. But my Dad would always be the sceptic.

He would ask what the sermon was about. Of course, I would always make it up.

But he always knew when I was lying. So sometimes it was better to go to the 40-minute service of Father McCarthy who held the local record for the fastest Mass. Canon Gahan was the longest one, sometimes lasting an hour and ten minutes.

Everything in our little town revolved around St Michael's Catholic Church. Whenever there was a funeral, the whole town came to a stand-still and people stood on the streets and crossed themselves as the hearse went by. People would walk behind the hearse and follow the coffin down to St Michael's for the burial. At every shop that the hearse passed by, the shopkeepers would systematically switch off the lights as a mark of respect. It was a close-knit community. For us, it was the cue to fill our pockets with sweets when the lights went out.

The mushroom farm, county council and the leather factory were the main employers, although the leather factory was already in de-cline and there was always high unemployment. So many men stood on the streets with nothing to do – known locally as 'corner boys'. Their 'job' was to prop up the buildings by leaning against them for five or six hours a day.

Suicide was common among farmers and rural workers. I remember at least three local suicides of our neighbours. The 1980s were a very tough time for everyone across the whole Republic of Ireland. Thursday was dole day and there were always large queues at the dole office. Then most of the men went to one of the thirteen pubs on the main street and drowned their sorrows.

The Catholic Church has seven sacraments – baptism, confession, first holy communion, confirmation, holy orders, marriage and the last rites.

I had no choice in baptism – I was baptised as a baby. As I grew up, I was told I was a Catholic. There was no discussion and we were not supposed to think for ourselves. So I went to the Catholic school and was brought up a Catholic. The seven sacraments were part of the rhythm of life in this part of the world, just like the pipes and the drums that stirred this little boy's heart. Everything was mapped out for us. All we had to do was obey the adults because they knew what was best for us.

Nuns and Brothers were part of the teaching staff at school and demanded unquestioning obedience. Deviation from the instructions was met with brutal punishment. I think the worst punishment was when we were made to kneel on two marbles and face the wall for two hours.

As I grew up I realised that only a few people in Gorey lived the good life. These tended to be professional people – doctors, policemen and, of course, the priests. These people seemed to live well in our town, while others spent the day walking the streets going nowhere. My Dad said, "Look at the police, the priests, the doctors. Learn from them. You don't see them spending all their money in the pub on Saturday night. You see them in church on Sunday. If you look to the 'corner boys', then you'll become one."

I was attracted to the Church. The drama of the Mass, the bells and smells, the choir, the processions, the robes – all this impressed me. As we grew up, we were instructed in our first confession and took our first communion, which was really just a fashion parade – the boys all wearing blazers and the girls turning up in white dresses and veils.

I was never interested in sport or stuff like that but I was interested in the Church. So my friends and I would hang around the local church and do small jobs for the priests, such as cleaning and gardening.

Forgiving Ferns

At St Michael's we were welcomed and encouraged by our parents and our neighbours. If we'd got into sport, we would have been running around in the pouring rain getting injured and being shouted at by the trainer. I was far happier involved in church life. I felt safe there.

The great day arrived when, at the age of 12, my friends and I were asked if we would like to be altar boys. This was a great privilege and I remember the way my Ma would proudly tell visitors about it. I'd always get a pat on the back and a 'well done'. This was much better than being in trouble, so I placed a high value on it.

Sometimes my Ma would talk as though I'd joined the priesthood, she was so proud. Actually, the thought did cross my mind. The priests did seem to live a good life, in a big house, and have the respect of the whole parish. And I was keen on the Church and the Masses.

Nearby, in Wexford, was St Peter's Seminary, where men would train for seven years to enter the priesthood. As life unfolded in this quiet part of Ireland, a man from our parish, Denis Byrne, was attending the seminary. He returned home, to Gorey, at weekends as our curate, Father William Roberts, was mentoring him. Denis Byrne lived near the church with his widowed mother, opposite Father Roberts's house.

We were a close-knit community and everyone knew everyone else, so it's difficult to say when I first met Denis Byrne. I do remember his father's funeral. The main street came to a standstill as usual. Denis Byrne walked behind the hearse with his mother. I noticed him because he was a striking character. He was tall with thick, dark hair and he had a very pronounced limp, as he was lame. He had a special shoe on one foot to make it easier for him to walk. He tended to always wear black clothes, even back then, as though he was preparing to be a priest.

One day, in 1983, my life changed. After school, I went to church to do some of my duties as an altar boy. I was in the altar boy vestry when I heard Father Byrne call me into the priest's vestry. This was quite normal as we often prepared things for the Mass.

Father Byrne gave me a damp cloth and asked me to clean the large black crucifix, which stood on a high window-sill. I went to get a chair to stand on but Father Byrne said he would lift me up. As he lifted me, I became aware that he was pushing his face into my genitals. The situation suddenly seemed a bit odd. After a while he put me down and said his foot was sore – as I said, he was lame in one of his legs.

He got a chair and knelt on it and told me to climb up and clean the window frames above the crucifix. As I did, he again pushed his face into my groin. This time he also fondled my buttocks and slipped a hand up my back, inside my clothes, and stroked me. I wasn't sure what was happening but something felt very wrong. As Father Byrne was a priest, it wasn't for me to question his behaviour. Life wasn't like that. We had to do what we were told to do by the adults. And do it without question.

At that moment, we heard a door bang and footsteps approaching. Father Byrne quickly ushered me to the sink and told me to wash it. I was confused by his urgency but did what I was told. As I looked across the room, I noticed Father Byrne pulling up the zip on his trousers and tucking in his shirt.

Canon Gahan, the parish priest, came into the vestry. He and Father Byrne talked briefly and then Canon Gahan left. As he did, Father Byrne turned off some of the lights in the corridor even though it was now starting to go dark.

It was about 4.30pm and he called me back to the chair and said he wanted to hear my confession. He said he would use anointing oil to forgive me and give me absolution for what I had done with him a few minutes earlier. I didn't really understand this. I wasn't aware that I had done anything with him, but that he had done something strange to me.

He started asking me if I had ever played with my penis or looked at naughty books with dirty pictures in. He said he had to pray for me and that I would receive a 'special anointing' if I told him my dirtiest thoughts.

He sat on the chair and pulled me onto his lap. He told me he had to practise hearing confession. He began whispering and blowing into my ear and asked me to talk about sex. He asked me if I had ever kissed a boy. I became very embarrassed and uncomfortable at this point and told him I hadn't. He asked me if I had ever kissed a girl. Again I replied, "No".

He then asked me if I had ever wondered what it would be like to kiss someone. He asked me a string of inappropriate questions – Did I masturbate? Did I fancy other altar boys? As he did so, he slipped his hand inside the back of my shirt. With his other hand he began stroking my legs. He was breathing very heavily.

He began kissing me and forced his tongue into my mouth. By now I felt completely numb with terror. I had no idea what was happening to

Forgiving Ferns

me, or why he was doing this, or if it was right or wrong. I asked him to stop but he refused.

He told me not to worry. "It will all be over in a few minutes. Then you will get a special blessing and a treat," he said. He stood me up and pulled my trousers down. He began masturbating me. Then he performed oral sex on me.

My heart was pounding with fear and confusion. He pulled his trousers down and forced me to give him oral sex. He grabbed the back of my head as he did. He began saying, "Receive the blessing, receive the blessing", over and over, as he ejaculated into my mouth. I felt like I was going to choke but he would not let go and kept saying, "Receive it!" He wouldn't release me until I swallowed.

Eventually he released my head and went to the sink to wash his hands and adjust his clothing. I was crying and felt very frightened of this man. He gave me a can of pop and told me to drink it. He stayed with me until I finished it. I felt trapped in the room by him.

He told me that I must tell no one what had happened. That it was just between the two of us. "If you tell anyone, there will be very severe consequences," he said. I decided to do as he said – he was a man of God and a priest. If I told anyone, who would believe my word over that of a priest? No one, not here in Gorey. He told me that what happened was 'normal' and that he did this to a lot of boys at St Peter's and they 'enjoyed it'.

He told me he would show me other things, which I would 'enjoy even more'. And he repeated that I must tell no one, otherwise severe consequences would happen. He also said, if I told anyone, I could no longer be an altar boy. After what seemed like an age, he finally left.

I remember at that moment thinking, who would believe me over a man of God? Priests hear everyone's confession. Everyone trusted them. There was no way I could have told anyone.

After Denis Byrne had left, I sat silently for several hours, trembling, alone in that dark little room. Fearful. Staring at the wall. I couldn't move. I felt transparent – as if you could see the guilt on my face, even though I had no real reason for feeling guilty.

After several hours, I finally made a move. I opened the church door quietly and slipped into the night. I could not go home the normal way because that would have meant passing Father Byrne's house. So I took a very long detour along the top road.

Back home, I met my brother and we went for a long bike ride through the darkness of the woods. We didn't speak. I had nothing to say. I thought, back then, that no one would ever hear this story. But now, at last, I have decided to tell my story. This is how it began. In darkness. Alone. Afraid. Abused.

Chapter 2

The Beast and the Beach

I think all abuse victims somehow hope and pray that the first encounter with abuse will be the last. Maybe it was a one-off, maybe it was all in their head. But abusers relish the control they have over others. And, as I discovered, it's never just a one-off. It's a complete lifestyle of controlling others. Before the abuse started, I was a young, good-natured boy. I was outgoing and adventurous. But all that had changed now.

One day, I was sitting at home and thinking, "The weekend is coming. The 'Beast' will be returning from St Peter's College." I was insecure and full of fear because he would almost always find a way of getting me. It was after the third or fourth time of being abused that I started to make an effort to avoid him. But avoiding him only made matters worse.

I quickly became accustomed to his methods. I knew that if I was early or on time for prearranged 'appointments' with him, then the

Forgiving Ferns

abuse would be gentle. But he would punish me if I was late or if I didn't smile and look like I was enjoying it, during the abuse. If I cried or looked away while he was forcing me to give him oral sex, he made things much more unpleasant.

My first lesson in how to get on the wrong side of him was when I was going to the church one afternoon, to help with some jobs. In order to get to the church, I had to pass by Denis Byrne's house. As I did, he came out of the door and saw me. He said, "Meet me at the back of the church tomorrow, after school, at four o'clock sharp."

On my way home from church, after helping out, I was thinking that I must not be late for him. It's best if I go to the shed at the back of the church and wait for him because he will hurt me if I am late. I thought there would be less chance of meeting anyone if I went straight there instead of going to school.

So, that day, I was playing truant from school because I simply could not focus on lessons. I was hanging about at the rear of the shed in the church grounds. The church stands near the main railway line to Dublin. Diesel engines passed there about six times a day. This was a place that interested young boys. We used to put stones on the tracks and watch the wheels shatter them. It seemed like fun.

So on this day, I occupied myself by reading the Dandy and the Beano. The old shed, behind the church, was semi-derelict. The windows were dirty and overgrown with ivy. Inside it was full of clutter, broken church furniture and a sad old statue of St Bridget. I put my school bag under a dusty old table. Then I sat there and waited.

Denis Byrne must have followed me because I was no sooner there than he had arrived. As soon as I saw him, my belly was in knots and I felt sick in my stomach, thinking about what he was going to do to me. He had a way of manipulating me and controlling me. Sometimes he would 'love bomb' me with nice words of acceptance. Other times he would give me money. On this occasion he had a fold-out camera and he took a photograph of me sitting in the shed with my school bag on the table.

He said he had all the evidence he needed to show to the headmaster, who was a Christian Brother, fond of using the leather and giving people six of the best. I knew I was in trouble. He told me to stand up and he stopped taking photographs. He lifted the broken door to close it. I was trapped.

He walked over to me, started to rub my penis through my trousers and said it was his turn to give me pleasure. He said that this was normal and that I would enjoy it. He said that I may not enjoy it at first but I would eventually. I was 12 years old. I was an innocent. I was not sexual. Yet he was certain that I would 'enjoy it'. It angered him when I told him I didn't like it.

He took a rolled-up newspaper from his trousers and knelt on it so as not to get dust on his uniform. He started rubbing my penis through my trousers. He was breathing heavily. He instructed me to come closer and I did, but at this stage all I was thinking of was being in big trouble with my teachers for bunking off school.

He took my trousers down and started to perform oral sex on me. I was crying and he told me to look at him and smile and if I didn't he would bite it off.

He did this for a while and then said that it was my turn. He told me that as he did this to me and had done me a favour, then I had to return the favour. I asked him not to come in my mouth and he promised me that he would not. I was forced to perform oral sex on him because, if I didn't, he would usually thump me.

Halfway through this traumatic ordeal he told me to stop. He reached over to the table, got some cardboard and put it on the ground and he told me to get down on all fours. He forced me to have anal sex. It was very painful and uncomfortable. He told me not to cry and that it would be over soon. As he forced himself into me, I let out a cry and he shouted at me, "I told you to be quiet. Now you will be sorry!"

So he forced his penis into me violently and I almost passed out with the pain. I lost control over my breathing. He kept it there for a few minutes then started to work on me very hard and fast.

I was crying, screaming, sweating and feeling sick. He was holding me tightly by the shoulders and it felt like he was killing me. I was trying to speak to tell him to stop but I couldn't get the words out. Every thrust took my breath away.

A train passed by, as he violently buggered me, and I focused on the train – trying to fix my thoughts on something else. I was now so sore, the pain was indescribable. I couldn't cry. As I started to scream he speeded up. As I cried, he punched me. As I begged him to stop, he told me to shut up.

He ejaculated into me and stayed there for a while thrusting into me, screaming, moaning, and holding my hips really tightly. Eventually he withdrew and stood up. I fell to the floor. All the energy left me. All my strength was gone. His face was very red and he was sweating. He gave me a five-pound note and he left the shed.

I learned not to cry after that. I realised crying didn't work. Crying didn't make him stop. Crying was for the weak. Crying was useless. Praying was useless. Being early or late for him was useless. No matter what methods I used to appease him, he did what he wanted to me, when he wanted to.

This was one of the most traumatic encounters which I had with Denis Byrne. It was difficult for me to think about that day. It was difficult to convey in writing and to be objective, and to this day, it is still so difficult. If you had trouble reading it, believe me, it is easier to read than to be that little, vulnerable, frightened boy.

Byrne left me there, freezing cold, semi-naked and bleeding from the backside. I felt traumatised, full of shame, neglected and unloved. Worst of all was feeling like I was to blame.

I believed that if I left this shed, people would look at me and know exactly what I had been up to. It was to take years to realise that it was not my shame or what I had been up to, but the abuse and criminal activity of this, so-called, man of the cloth.

He did this to me, yet I felt as though I was the one doing the wrong. It was the way he confused me and twisted the facts – using a camera and the fact I was in the wrong for bunking off school – that made me feel responsible. It took years of painful lessons to show me that I was a child below the age of consent. That I was not sexual in any way. That the abuser was the one in the wrong. I know that now. But then, as a child, I remember feeling that it was my fault, that I had, in some bizarre way, brought this on myself. It was hours before I left that shed.

Denis Byrne continued to abuse and rape me this way many times until he was ordained in 1987 and was moved to a neighbouring parish, then to a parish in Shrewsbury in the UK.

He left my head in such a mess, I had no working knowledge of sex and relationships. I didn't understand what was happening to me or why it was happening. I eventually began to accept from him that what he was doing to me was love and then logically, in my weak mind, I began to see it as consensual. I felt guilty for years after. Why had I kept returning to the shed and to the grounds of St Michael's, under his instruction, where he would commit similar acts upon me?

My mind and my body was a blank sheet of paper on which, for three years, he scrawled his lies in large letters. My life had been a brand-new exercise book and this bully had defaced every page before I ever got to write in it myself. He completely dominated my life. He told me I was gay. That if I wasn't gay then I would not be able to do these things with him. But, looking back now, I was not doing things 'with' him, he was doing things 'to' me. I was below the age of consent. I was a child. He was the adult.

Back then I believed his lies. I had no idea, despite his uncaring brutality, that this so-called 'man of the cloth' was nothing but a dangerous sexual predator who stole my innocence.

Somehow I became 'accustomed' to being abused and raped over that three-year period. In a way, though it may be hard for others to understand, it became 'normal'. And I felt that it no longer troubled me. This is how human beings often 'cope' with trauma – we tell ourself that what's happening to us is 'normal'.

The beach at Courtown harbour was one of the most beautiful places I knew. In the wintertime, it was a great place of solitude and peace.

Often, after a session of abuse, I would walk the three miles down the road to this place of beauty. Somehow the breathtaking views and the solitude calmed my troubled soul. The soft, sandy beaches were my friend. The starlit sky my counsellor. The gentle rhythm of the waves, falling onto the beach, told me there was more to life. The changing seasons gave me hope – that there would be another season in my life without such pain. That the harsh winter in my heart would one day give way to spring. That beach convinced me that there was something beyond the depravity of life in Gorey.

It was here, on this shore, that I fantasised about running away to England to escape my sorry existence. Anywhere would have been better than having to face the dark corridors of St Michael's church and the convent grounds. The bells of the church could be heard across the town, instructing people to say the Angelus at noon and six o'clock. It seemed there was no escape from that place. But down here, in Courtown Harbour, looking out to sea, reliving the horror in my mind, I dared to believe there was something better for me. I believed that one day I would escape the darkness and the pain of this place.

"We think sometimes that poverty is only being hungry, naked and homeless. The poverty of being unwanted, unloved and uncared for is the greatest poverty. We must start in our own homes to remedy this kind of poverty."

Mother Teresa

Chapter 3

Like a Thief in the Night

I'm sad to say I believed the lies that the abuser told me. I responded sexually to his advances – it was easier than fighting him off. After three years of his manipulation, I eventually believed him when he told me I was gay. Believing what was happening to me was 'normal' was easier than fighting it. The transition from being sexually abused by a man and beginning to live a gay lifestyle is surprisingly easy. Meeting other young boys who had been told the same lies and had the same experiences, we found our puberty had now kicked in and we were having sexual feelings of our own. I gave myself over to homosexuality and it gladly accepted me.

After Denis Byrne was ordained to the priesthood, in August 1987, and shipped off to the diocese of Shrewsbury, I began to feel free of his control. By the time he left, I was fully inducted into the homosexual life-style. I had many encounters with boys my own age – experimenting at the back of the railway station or in the fields. These encounters carried on through to adult life.

Sexual education was introduced into Catholic schools in a new government initiative to make kids aware of teenage pregnancies.

Other kids thought it was naughty to smoke behind the bike shed. Yet here was I, in fulblown sexual relationships with men, and boys my own age. I felt superior in some strange way.

I never saw anything wrong with my secret gay lifestyle. It grew on me. I had no interest in girls – I never had an encounter with any of them. But my confidence in my secret sex life and my peace with my sexuality was soon to be challenged.

I was 15 years old and still at school. During the school holidays I worked at the mushroom farm. It was hard work for little pay but it was fun to get up at five o'clock in the morning and walk into the countryside, up Creagh Hill, to the mushroom farm. I'd work till one o'clock, or so, then go to the local take-away and peel twenty stones of potatoes. Then I had to put the lot through a machine and turn them into chips – all for an amazing £25 per week.

At that time, my brother Pat was offered a

job in England. He would be working with a road construction company. It was a big thing, for a country bumpkin like my brother, to go off to the UK. He broke the news to my Mum and Dad giving them about ten minutes' notice that he was leaving. He didn't even say goodbye.

My Dad was concerned, as any parent would be. He knew the UK. He knew London, Glasgow, Manchester and Birmingham were very lonely, and sometimes hostile places to be for a young Irishman. These were the days of war and the mainland bombings. This troubled my Dad and he was so upset that Pat was leaving. But he let him go because what future would he have in Gorey or anywhere else in Ferns? It was work in the UK or become a 'corner boy'.

Frank Keegan came for my brother at five o'clock in the evening. He arrived in a fancy four-wheel-drive jeep to take my brother to the UK. My Dad was very sad to see him go. He had spent twenty-five years there, at the time when the 'NINA' (No Irish Need Apply) sign was in the window of every flat and digs in the UK. He knew that joining an Irish centre was the only way to get along, and that meant getting in with the wrong crowd. Irish Centres were full of workmen and if my brother was not strong-willed, he would soon be influenced by political activists. My brother left Ireland and I never had a chance to say good-bye to him.

That evening my Mum, Dad, my oldest brother David and Chris, my cousin, walked down to Main Street. It was Corpus Christi – a religious celebration in which Catholic priest,s and the Legion of Mary, would parade a Monstrance through the town and we would all go to the church for a Benediction service held by the Canon. Then the pipe band and the brass band would play on the streets.

My Dad suffered from asthma. He had to retire early from the farm he was working on, after some bales of hay fell on him and some cattle crushed him. He was never the same again. Sometimes he was moody and grumpy, probably because of fatigue and ill-health.

On the way home from the procession of Corpus Christi, he had to sit on the wall of the theatre, as he was wheezy and out of breath. Mum said his asthma was triggered by anxiety. We called the doctor and he came to visit. As usual, he put Dad on a nebulizer and steroids and things settled down.

That evening I took a glass of goat's milk up to the bedroom to my Dad. Goat's milk is excellent for asthmatics. As I took it to him I saw he had been crying and I asked him what was wrong. He told me that Pat's trip would all end in tears. It was a bit disturbing as I had never seen my Dad cry. I felt for him and I started to cry. I was sad as well. So I sat with him and we talked for a while. Then I put a question to him, "If I told you something about me, would you be mad?"

He said, "No. What's the matter?"

I told him that Father Byrne and I had done things with each other and that I was not sure how I felt about women.

With hindsight, my timing could have been better. My Dad was distraught that his son, of the same name, had left the country. On the same evening he'd had a major asthma attack. And now his youngest son was having the 'I think I'm gay' chat!

I talked and he listened, patiently. He asked me how long it had been going on. He asked me where. He asked me what we did. I couldn't answer that question. I was too ashamed. But I told him enough for him to understand. He asked me if I wanted any of this to happen. I said, "Not at first."

He said, "I will deal with this tomorrow. Go to bed. You've got to be up at five o'clock for work."

I didn't know what he meant by 'deal with it tomorrow'. Deal with who? With me? I was a bit anxious about it all. I lay in bed and could hear my Mum and Dad talking for ages in the next room.

Next morning I left early for the mushroom farm. I worked in the dark packing sacks of manure till about eight-thirty when we stopped for a coffee break. After drinking my coffee, I went back to work in the shed. My cousin, Liam Egan, came to the shed and called me out.

This was a bit unusual and I wondered what he wanted. He just blurted it out, "You have got to come home with me now. Your father is dead." There was no emotion, no hug, no 'I'm sorry, son'. Just the facts.

Hearing your father has died would be a shock to anyone – I experienced that. But on top of that, the words of Denis Byrne leapt into my mind. He'd told me many times, after abusing me, "If you ever tell anyone about this, there will be severe consequences."

Last night I'd told my Dad what had happened and now he'd died. These were very severe consequences. I was sure I was to blame for my Dad's death.

We got into Liam's yellow Vauxhall Viva,

along with my brother David. I sat in the back panicking and thinking, "They're all going to blame me. I am responsible. I am to blame."

I couldn't believe my Dad could drop dead just six hours after I told him about Denis Byrne. Death had come like a thief in the night. I didn't really know how I was feeling but I knew this – I was to blame for my father's death. It was as if Denis Byrne, though far away in England, still had power to control my life.

Chapter 4

Men in Black

After a silent journey from the mushroom farm, we arrived home. Life seemed to have gone into slow motion. We had to wait outside the house while the undertaker removed my father's body. There was a temporary coffin in the hallway. We waited outside for about ten minutes. I didn't think to walk round to the back door. I didn't want to walk to the back door. I was very frightened to see a dead body.

In a close-knit Irish community like ours, when someone dies, you draw all the curtains in the house. You don't celebrate Christmas that year. You don't put up Christmas trees or decorations. You open the front window, where the person died, to let his spirit out. Well that's what happened here. A bit of superstition mixed with our culture. Then the community sandwich brigade turns up with teas, cakes and sandwiches. The whole community gets involved.

Eventually, I went into the house and looked at my mother. She was clearly shaken. I didn't hug her or talk to her. I looked at her, surrounded by our neighbours and Father William Roberts.

I was unsure of what to do or say, or how to behave. I had no idea how to handle it. Then I suddenly thought, we needed to get hold of my brother Pat in England. We didn't have a phone in the house so we went to the local police station and gave them my brother's address. They sent a telegram to inform him of the situation.

That evening the police turned up at the house, said they had contacted my brother and he was returning home. They also said that my Dad had to be taken to Wexford General Hospital for a post mortem.

The next day, my uncle Bill took me to see my Dad. We went to Gorey District Hospital and found the mortuary. The ward sister gave my uncle Bill the key to the mortuary so we could see my Dad. We nervously opened the door. My heart was beating fast. There, in the room was my Dad's body. This was the first time I'd seen him since I'd told him about the abuse. His tongue was all swollen up and his face was purple and blue. My uncle, who had seen death many times when he was in the navy, said, "When you come back tonight for evening prayers, his body will be much paler."

My brother Pat returned home and I went to

his bedroom to see him. There was no hug, no hello, he was just there crying about what had happened. I couldn't cry. Crying didn't work. Crying was not going to bring him back. I thought if I cried, then it would get worse. I had been programmed to function under stress. Programmed to focus on other things. Programmed to suppress my feelings at the drop of a hat. Denis Byrne taught me how to do that.

That night, we marched behind the hearse to St Michael's. As I had seen many times before, the lights in the shops went off as we passed and people stood and watched us pass. The whole town came to a standstill. Behind us was my mum with auntie Lucy and auntie Jean in the mourners' car.

My Dad's remains were placed in St Michael's Cemetery overlooking the church and the railway station. As we stood around the grave, all dressed in black, listening to the prayers of the priest, it began to rain. In the corner of the churchyard, I could see the shed where Father Byrne first buggered me. And I felt the fear and shame all over again. Now he had even robbed me of the right to cry at my father's funeral. That's all I could think about as they lowered my Dad into the ground. I had told my Dad the secret of what happened in that shed and now the severe consequences were unfolding before my eyes. I couldn't cry but the raindrops may have been the tears of God.

After the funeral, we returned home where the sandwich brigade had done their work - loads of coffee, tea and ham sandwiches in the front living-room.

At that time, I had a cast on my arm for a broken finger. I'd had a fight with my brother and been injured in the fight. I'd had it for about three weeks before my Dad died.

My Mum looked really tired. Father Roberts popped in to say the rosary with her, for what seemed like an age. My Mum was talking about something important with him and they stopped talking as soon as I came into the room. I had interrupted them and he left soon after. I assumed she was telling him about the abuse.

It was time for me to make a trip back to Wexford hospital to get the cast removed from my hand. I left my Mum on the downstairs bed, where my older brother slept. She looked so tired. She lay down and I said I was going down town.

It was late evening by the time I got home. As I came in the house, I was surprised that my

Mum was still there, in the same position I had left her that morning. I thought she must have been really tired after the funeral and slept the whole day. I didn't want to disturb her. I thought I'd let her catch up on her sleep, so that evening I went to Wexford.

I went for a few days with my friend David and stopped in a village at Larkin's Cross, just outside Wexford Town. My appointment was 8.30am the next morning.

We stayed the night at Rudolph's house. He was the brother of Roberto Rubertino, who owned the take-away where I worked.

I got a call there from my brother David. He called to say that our Mum was in hospital for a few days' rest. I thought nothing of it – a few days would be good for her. But David insisted I go and see her.

Next day, I went to get my hand x-rayed and they decided to remove the cast from my arm, as the break had healed up. I had to book a separate next-day appointment for that.

I went to the department where my mother was. I found her there asleep. I talked to my Mum, to try and get her to wake up, but she didn't respond. So I called the nurse who said she would be with me in a few moments. I left my Mum asleep and waited outside the office with my best friend David. After what seemed an age, a young nurse came out to talk to me. She mentioned words like 'coma', 'stroke', 'cardio vascular accident', and 'unlikely to wake up'. She made me a cup of tea but I didn't realise that she was trying to prepare me for my mother's death.

I went home to Gorey and told my brothers the details. We went back to Wexford General Hospital where we visited our Mum, late at night, with family friends. We got home and we prayed in the house and said the rosary for my Mum.

The next day I had to go back to Wexford Hospital to get the cast removed from my hand. It was a scorching hot day. The cast was removed. I thought that, as I was with my friend David, we would both go and visit my Mum after we left our luggage at Larkin's Cross, where we would stay a few days to be near Mum. So I didn't go to see my Mum just then. I went to Larkin's Cross to drop the luggage off.

Later that day we were playing with Rudolph's Rottweiler at his house when Rudolph turned up in his little yellow mini. I thought, "He's home early".

He got out of his car and stood there looking at me, still holding the car door open. He said,

"Noel..." There was a pause. I looked at him and felt strange. "Your Mum is dead," he said.

Denis Byrne had cursed me again and, this time, I could barely stand up. I could not cry. I went inside and Paulo broke the news to the rest of the family I was staying with. They all broke down in tears even though they hardly knew my Mum. All I could do was sit with my back to the open fireplace and place my hands on my head and stare blankly at the floor. After a while they took me to see my Mum at the hospital.

On arrival there we met our aunt Morag, who came from Dudley, in England. She had flown over and set herself a place to stay in our home, whilst she and her husband tried to help in some way. But she was a stumbling block to me.

She sternly criticised me for not putting my Mum first – for delivering my luggage to Larkin's Cross rather than visiting my Mum first. Then she said God would be very disappointed in me and that I would never see my Mum again.

She took me to the hospital bed where Mum was wrapped in white sheets. She tried to unravel the sheets to reveal her face but I wouldn't let her. I refused to look at my Mum's face on her deathbed. I don't know why. Perhaps because deep down I felt that I had broken the covenant with Denis Byrne and felt cursed. That I was responsible for my parents' deaths – for bringing on the family the severe consequences I'd been warned about.

From that moment on, I knew I could never tell anyone about the abuse or about the deaths of my parents. I was silenced and Denis Byrne's control on me was working, despite him being a thousand miles away in a different country.

That evening my mother's body was moved to St Michael's Church. Three days later, on a Sunday morning, after the 11.30am Mass, her body was taken to the graveyard and laid to rest in the same grave as my father. History was repeating itself, as I looked at the church and the shed where all this began. This time I did manage to cry – but only for a brief moment.

I thought, "What have I done?" My parents were excellent role models. They attended church regularly. They went on pilgrimages. They were generous-kind-hearted people. They didn't deserve this.

I felt totally responsible. I felt all the guilt, all the shame, and yet there was not a person in the world I could tell.

I thought, in that indoctrinated brain of mine, that not even God would listen to me. But there was one person who would listen to me, and it wasn't God. Those ten days broke me. But they were also to make me.

Chapter 5

Niamh

"What is a friend? A single soul in two bodies."

   Aristotle (384 - 322BC)

My uncle Bill was a wise man who had fore-sight. My aunt Morag had come out of the blue to Gorey, from England. She hadn't come when my Mum needed her most – when my father died. She came the day before my Mum died.

There had been some shenanigans in my Mum's family. My Mum and her sisters had grown up in our house and as my Mum was the last one to get married, she and my Dad paid off the mortgage and continued living there until they died. The house was in my mother's maiden name, 'Egan'. And I remember a day aunt Morag told us off – that we must respect 'her home', when she returned back to the UK. It seemed that she had been planning to take ownership of the house after my mother's death.

My uncle Bill, who lived just across the street, took my older brother to the solicitors' office and secured the deeds to the property. When the solicitors heard from my uncle Bill about the plotting of my relatives, they decided that we had the right to the property. We obtained legal ownership despite the property being in my Mum's maiden name. Legal ownership was transferred to us.

My brother David settled the argument of ownership with aunt Morag by producing the title deeds. She got really angry that he had been to the solicitors' office with my uncle Bill and secured ownership. She returned to the England three days after the funeral of my Mum. To this day we have never seen or heard from her again. Not even a Christmas card.

Apart from my uncle Bill and cousin Chris, across the street, and my aunts Maureen and Pat, who lived on a farm on the Arklow Road, we had no one. My brothers and I were free. We had the house to ourselves.

We had no parents around so we did what many teenagers left to their own devices would do. We ran riot – 'sex and bikes and rock and roll'. We became the neighbours from hell. I suppose it was our way of dealing with the pain.

Within a year of my parents' death, they had organised one of the largest motorbike gangs in the land and ran it from our home. We were getting attention because we had a town house with a large garden. My brother had an interest in motor mechanics. People used to bring bikes to him to get them repaired. He had a real gift. Eventually he went on to win the Motor Bike Mechanic of the Year award.

He got a job in repairs and fitting in a motorbike company on Main Street and he soon became the most trusted, hard-working, motorbike repair specialist in the area. He had the qualifications, the tools and the facilities to back it up. Our house rapidly became a drop-in centre for motorbike health checks.

My other brother David, became, the leader of a private army of bikers from all around the country. He got a reputation and became known across Ireland and was greatly feared. They called him 'The Grunt' because of his communication skills. When you asked him a question, he would grunt the answer.

My brother Pat was known as 'The Black Flash' because he always wore black oily overalls. If you were ever in our street you would see The Black Flash road-testing some old bike but all you would see was a black flash as he roared past.

They used to tease me and call me 'Lofty'

because I was tall, though my brothers said it was because I had no brain upstairs. As far as I could work it out, I think I was the brains of the bunch – they were the brawn.

Several bikers' clubs flocked to our house. One night, a large group of bikers stopped over at our house. Unfortunately for him, a local burglar broke into our home that night and faced so many violent, armed and angry bikers. It turned out to be a man who used to bully us when we were at school together. He was always in trouble with the police. But he really regretted breaking into our house that night. Breaking into the house was easy. Breaking out not so easy, confronted by the guys. I never heard of him breaking the law again – I think he felt lucky to escape with his life.

In the middle of all this chaos and violence, I developed a love of helping people. I was part of the Red Cross, the Civil Defence and the Auxiliary Fire Service, all voluntary organisations. I took part in ambulance courses and first aid courses and even mountain rescue. I had a real appetite for helping people. Deep down I suppose I became a people-pleaser. Bizarrely, I missed Denis Byrne saying all those nice things about me. It was weird and I have yet to work that one out. But people will believe anything from a priest. And, one way or another, I think we all look for affirmation in life.

My brothers continued to pursue a life of bikes and booze. Arguments were always solved very quickly and before long people knew who was in charge. At first, the bike clubs were a great asset to raising money for charities such as Cancer Research. They were looked upon as harmless and most of them were honest, decent people, though there was always a small criminal element to the group. Unfortunately, people started dying in 'road accidents'. People were murdered. Men went 'missing'. There were shootings, major police investigations and firearm incidents across the country. All the investigations into the crimes led only to one conviction. The Irish Garda didn't have a dedicated murder team in their ranks.

The bike clubs soon lost the support of the public but by then they didn't care. My brothers had their new-found family. They had their bikes, booze and their 'bitches', as the girls were referred to.

I was a punchbag at times, but nothing really hurt me. The words, the verbal abuse, the fights I had with my older brother, the punches, the flying saucepans – I felt nothing. No one ever hurt me like Denis Byrne.

There were times when I would have an adolescent screaming fit, shouting at the mirror – telling myself I was a failure and useless. I usually smashed something up during those mad outbursts. My poor neighbours were horrified to see objects flying out of the windows. But, sadly, these are the effects of anger turned inward.

My brothers had their 'hobby'. They had their booze, their women and their status as men to be feared and respected. There were times I would just tag along with my first aid kit to a bikers' rally and just wait for the fighters to come to my tent for treatment for nosebleeds or to bandage their knuckles.

I became accustomed to it. I became immune to seeing legs and faces getting broken and seeing stab wounds. I didn't care. My feelings of pity and my emotions left on the day my parents died.

I was known around the town as the quiet one, the shy one. I was the one who didn't succumb to the temptations of booze, bikes, murder and crime. At least, that was always the impression I gave. In reality, and to my shame, I worked many times behind the scenes, travelling to the UK, Amsterdam, Dublin and Belfast, exchanging cash for guns. It had started when one of the bikers died in a road accident. His brother had given me the box from the back of his motorbike. He had rescued it before the police had arrived. He asked me to 'keep it safe'. Curious as to what it contained I'd had a peek inside. It was full of guns. It was a dangerous game, risking a long jail sentence if caught but there was always a market for weapons in those days. Not a lot of people knew my secret life. I don't know what it was about secrets and me. They seemed to follow me everywhere.

If the bike club had known I was living a gay lifestyle, they would have completely rejected me. Believe me, I thought long and hard about showing my brothers up by embarrassing them – telling everyone I was gay. I didn't do that just yet. My brothers had their bikes. I had my homosexuality. That's all I cared about until one day the confusion set in. I met a woman...

Her name was Niamh (pronounced 'Neave') and she put a big spanner in the works. She was 16 years old, the same age as me. She was lovely, blonde and petite. I had known her from a very young age. She was at an adventurous age and into Slayer, Meatloaf, ACDC and all that 'thrash' I used to listen to.

One day she asked me if I would take her to Johnny Eagle's, in Dublin, for a tattoo. So I said, "Why not?" We formed a deep friendship. She shared some deep hurts from the past and I told her some things about my past. She became a real soul-friend. A few weeks later, we were making love in my bedroom. It was weird being with a woman. The whole time I was confused in my head. I became insecure about my sexuality. I was unsure why I was able to do this with a woman, when a priest had told me I was gay.

But there was something special about Niamh and it wasn't just the sex. It was the fact that she trusted me with her whole life and what she had been through. And I shared with her about my encounters with Denis Byrne. We made love many times but we always talked and we cared for each other. Then the wrestle began as to whether or not I was gay.

I was no longer at peace with myself and who I was. I didn't accept a bisexual scenario, I refused to accept it. There is gay and there is straight – choose one or the other, you can't do both. I couldn't live with being caught between the two. Either I was gay or I was straight.

Really what my soul was crying out for was not sex but, friendship, truth and honesty. I had that in Niamh until her family circumstances suddenly got worse. She ran away from home in 1989. I lost contact with her and was really sad when she went. I felt I had lost part of myself. I went through a sort of bereavement, not knowing where she was and unable to contact her.

Niamh had shown me something. She had shown me a world of heterosexuality which seemed to undermine what Denis Byrne had instilled in me. I was no longer confident that 'homosexual' was who I really was. And it really bothered me.

In some ways, this inner confusion was worse than the abuse. There were times I wished Denis Byrne would come back and instruct me again. My parents weren't here any more. I had no cues and no guidance. Left alone by a bunch of bikers who only sought to serve themselves, there was no care, no love at home any more. Not the love and care that was shown to me by Niamh. She had done something to my soul and I didn't know if I should kill her for it or thank her for it. I was hurting and alone again. Without hope and without God in the world.

Chapter 6

The Lady and the Lorry

The police arrived at the house one morning asking for me. They may have been calling about any number of things – illegal weapons, beatings, dodgy motorbikes. Between us we'd probably been involved in all of them. So I was glad when they asked about Niamh. She had been reported missing and police had found her secret diary under her bed. The diary listed most of our sexual encounters and also included details of my abuse by Denis Byrne. However, not once did they ask about him or the abuse.

I was desperate to know her whereabouts too but couldn't think how to help the police. I put the word out to the guys and we managed to find out who she ran away with. They traced her and found her. But she told her parents she wasn't coming back. She never wrote to me and never explained but she didn't have to. I knew for her it was leave or die. She left and lived for a while. I had her address and I knew she was relatively safe. That's all that mattered to me.

At that time, I would probably have killed anyone who tried to harm her. All this gave me the thought that running away was not a bad idea.

I found myself in moments of solitude, down at Courtown Harbour, sitting on the dunes looking out across the sea to England. When I came to the shores of Ireland, I found some space for reflection and hope in this place. Part of me wondered, "What if I went further? What if I went far away? Maybe I could find peace. Maybe I would find some healing for my troubled soul."

Yet again I suppressed my emotions and hid things deep inside. I refused to admit to myself that I was hurting. I tried to get over Niamh leaving and move on. I was unsure if I should emigrate or to go and live in Dublin. I had no parents to help me now. I had grown up and been programmed to do as I was told by the adults. But now the adults were gone and there was no one to tell me what to do.

I had enough money from the sale of illegal firearms and knives to keep me going but I wanted to do something meaningful.

Deep down I felt I was good-natured, caring and considerate. Denis Byrne hadn't taken that from me. Not permanently anyway.

The Red Cross, the Civil Defence and Auxiliary Fire Service were the only normal things in my life. I knew I was living this bizarre double life – I mixed with the police and ambulance crews. I was well known in polite society but led this secret life of gay sex and gun smuggling. The gossip about my brothers increased. Talk about the crimes, the murders, the biker shootings and violence were not helpful.

The respectable people I knew were becoming worried that I was part of an increasingly violent group. The gangs my brothers were part of were fiercely competitive. They wanted to take over everything and run the whole show. But for me, I just wanted to make some money here and there.

Before long I was making trips to Belfast to 'help' people with some bad investors. But I wanted out of punishment beatings and violence. The gay lifestyle was more appealing and more pleasurable.

I felt life had cast me on an ocean of uncertainty without a compass. I was hungry for direction. Although I was now an adult myself, I often found myself wondering when the grown-ups would come and tell us what to do.

One day I found some direction in a large

farmer called John Harvey, who owned the newsagent's and grocer's shop near the top of the main street in Gorey. He was six feet tall and almost as wide. As I chatted to him in his shop, he seemed like a corner boy – knowing about a lot of things – but he stood inside the shop not outside. He had studied art at De la Salle in Waterford. His family was Protestant so I was a bit cautious of him. I'd go into his shop to get some cigarettes. He'd ask me if I'd ever read the Bible. I'd say, "Not too many pages". We'd always chat about God or the Bible or something along those lines whenever I went in.

One day, I was coming out of the doctor's surgery, opposite John's shop, after visiting the doctor. I saw a woman push a small child out of the way of a moving truck, only to be run over by the truck herself. She saved the little boy's life but she was trapped under the truck. She was in bad shape. A group of us tried hard to free her. We tried resuscitating her. We tried everything I knew from my Red Cross training but she died right there in the road. Eventually the police and ambulance came and took her body away. I was sorry for her but even things like this didn't really move me any more. It was almost automatic now to suppress my emotions in stressful situations.

The following day I went into John's shop and I picked up a paper and started to read about the accident. The newspaper said the lady died on the way to hospital but she died under the truck. I know, I knelt beside her in the road and watched her go. John said he knew a man who died in place of another man just like that lady.

He told me about a meeting he attended at Arklow, in Riverwalk tearooms. He invited me to hear about this chap who died in someone else's place. He said they usually arrived about 7.30pm, for tea and biscuits, and then read a little from the Bible. Then they would discuss the Bible. I was ready for a bit of fun. I thought I would tear their beliefs to shreds or, at least, I would have a look at this little secret meeting and see what was in it for me. I was bored and at that time in my life, ignorant to the fact that I was about to exchange one set of problems for another.

Chapter 7

Riverwalk Tearooms

Riverwalk Tearooms, in Arklow, is a quaint place from a bygone era. Nestled between the road bridge and the steep hillside, the tearooms seemed to have been there for ever. A small flotilla of wooden rowing boats, moored together, bobbed on the river outside. I remember the first meeting I went to with John Harvey and his Protestant friends there. I didn't realise it at the time but there was something almost baptismal about coming down to the river to think about God.

John was a farmer who lived on the outskirts of the town. His farm was situated a few miles from his home. He kept sheep and cows and he owned a small newsagent's. Although I knew he was a Protestant, I never understood much about his faith. John invited me to this meeting and I was keen to go and see what they got up to. I liked the idea of a group of people who didn't meet in a church or wear collars and who didn't have all the bells and smells I was used to. It seemed free and non-religious.

It was a Tuesday evening. John had an old silver Toyota saloon and the heater didn't work. The drive over to Riverwalk Tearooms was a cold one but we talked about, my parents, the bikers and the Red Cross. John was a good listener. More of a true friend than anyone I had come across.

We arrived at the tearooms and to my amazement I found out that it was owned by one of my former schoolteachers. There were people there from the town – people who I knew locally. I was amazed by all these people meeting in a darkened coffee shop, out of hours, to read and discuss the Bible. It seemed almost subversive.

John presented me with a brand-new NIV study Bible. It was worth about £30 at the time. I was impressed and it made me feel valued. John and I had many conversations about his faith and he proved to be a good communicator of the Gospel and the God he believed in.

The group were very welcoming. I saw my former teacher in a very different light to when he was teaching me. He was friendlier and spoke with me on a level playing field, rather than the way he used to teach me. I could see a very clear difference in him. He used to be very authoritarian, very intimidating and often would use the cane. But he had changed. Perhaps because he was no longer teaching or because he was following his dream of owning his own business. Or perhaps the change was because his faith had changed him. I was very interested indeed. My former teacher seemed to be a changed man.

We sat down and he made some lovely tea and produced some scrumptious fruit scones. They started the meeting in true Brethren style. There were no instruments, no guitars and no worship leader. Just a bunch of men and women who sang two songs – 'There is a Redeemer' and 'Make me a channel of your peace'.

'Make me a channel of your peace' was a challenging song. I wasn't ready for peace in my mind. I was still at war with myself. And St Francis of Assisi happened to be Catholic. These Protestants were singing the words of a Catholic. This bit of the meeting didn't make sense to my sectarian mind.

There was no altar to lay the Bible down on or fancy white cloths, no gloves used to turn the pages. The Bibles they used were all scribbled on and highlighted. I thought, "You sacrilegious bunch of Bible vandals!" They were literally Bible bashers – some Bibles were in total tatters. "Oh, if the Mother Superior knew they were writing and highlighting their Bibles, there would be war!" I thought.

When the main man of the evening started to share from the Scripture, I was amazed. His name was Herbert Harper. The owner of Avoca Manor, he was an Englishman. He spoke from Romans chapter three, verse twenty-three: 'All have sinned and fallen short of the glory of God.' He went on to talk about the wages of sin being death but the free gift of God was eternal life.

He spoke about justification, explaining it as 'Just-as-if-I-have-never-sinned'. Herbert knew his Bible and I was squaring up to him.

I thought if I asked a difficult question like "Why do babies die?" then he would have the answer. But, instead, I thought I wouldn't do battle with him yet. And I was wise not to, he too used to be a schoolteacher, far more intelligent than I would ever be. I knew I was out of my depth but I was interested to know more. I was open and I was keen to keep coming on these Tuesdays.

With my religious upbringing I was not opposed to the teachings in the Bible. I was wide-open to discuss and explore. I was not one of those people who thought that I would never read the Bible or go to church. I was interested and deep down I was searching for peace in my heart.

I began a real relationship with John Cobbe and attended the meetings in the tearooms and often talked in his shop in between customers coming in and out.

Catholicism is based around the seven sacraments. John started a Bible study on this. He showed me the biblical principle of baptism and contrasted it with the teaching of the Catholic Church. From Scripture he was able to show me that the teachings of the Catholic Church were far from the teachings of the Apostle Paul.

The teachings of the Bible seemed real and more truthful than those of Catholicism. The teachings would agree with my head. I would say that, at this time, only my head was converted. The teachings would take a little longer to drop eighteen inches into my heart.

He argued with me about various teachings. I argued about other religions. Most important of all, he explained the crucifixion. This started to intrigue me. I had never really known the full teachings of Christianity. In Catholicism we were encouraged to read the writings of Padre Pio or Mother Theresa. Reading the Bible and thinking for yourself was not encouraged. Virtually all the readings and the adoration of the saints were promoted, except personal reading of the Bible. Why is that?

Every evening I would pop up to the shop when John arrived after milking the cows. We would talk. He would listen. A customer would come and go. We would continue to talk. I had found some meaning in the madness but that was all I had found.

I think logically this faith made more sense. I discovered more about Jesus in one Tuesday night meeting that I ever did in a lifetime of going to Catholic Mass. Surely, there was something wrong in the Catholic Church. Surely, there was something right about this Jesus. I kept visiting John.

Before long I had made a mediocre attempt at being a Christian. I am sure I failed miserably every day but I tried. However, an academic conversation about religion will never carry you through the difficult times. The Gospel had to move to my heart.

Chapter 8

Dark Night of the Soul.

Some time later I decided that moving to Dublin would be a good idea. I went there with a friend. We found a nice cottage on Rings End Row, opposite the Point Depot on the docks. During this time, I earned my money working at various jobs, mainly as a porter in the hospital.

I went for a walk in Tara Street, in Dublin, and was passing by the fire station. A few doors up was a place called The Lighthouse and then St Mark's Family Worship Centre. Next door was the cult awareness centre, then the Chinese Christian Fellowship and then Grace Baptist Church. "There must be Bible studies galore in Dublin," I thought.

I went into the Lighthouse which was owned by Jim Hannah. We spent a lot of time talking about stuff and on Saturday nights I would go to the Bible studies there. On Sunday mornings, I would go to Irish Town Gospel Hall, a very serious Brethren group and very exclusive. They had lots of rules. Yet I found it interesting and I was always impressed to hear people talk about Jesus the way they did. It was a total contrast to my Catholic upbringing. I learned a little about Catholicism, Hinduism, and false religions. It was exciting to be able to go and listen to the sermons. That was until one day they started to speak against homosexuality and said it was a sin. I found that very offensive, it didn't settle well with me.

I was trying to avoid the issue of my sexuality because I was still confused about how I managed to function sexually with Niamh. I had no parents to guide me. So I spoke to the preacher, after the service. He told me he found homosexuality absolutely abhorrent. I couldn't see why he had such a problem with it. It was like there was fog in my thinking. I couldn't relate to what he was saying at all. As far as I was concerned, homosexuality was fun and harmless. I thought, "Stuff him, if he doesn't want people like me in his church."

I started to see a different side to the church so I left there and I went to The Fellowship Bible Church on Abbey Street, which was next to the Salvation Army. I went there too, one night, for a laugh. It was great to see all the trumpets and the brass stuff.

Fellowship Bible Church was much newer than Irish Town Gospel Church. I thought that it would have a different view on homosexuality. I tried to avoid the issue because I liked going there and it was great to see drummers, percussionists, violins and guitars all going at the same time. The worship and singing were really exciting and full of life. I attended there for a few months.

One night a man stood up in the meeting and shared the story of his life. He told the congregation that God had delivered him from the pain of being abused. He said he was sexually abused when he was younger. Before long I counted over thirty people who stood up in support of him and they all claimed that they too were abused and they were raped – some by family members, others in scout halls, others in churches. They were all condemning what had happened to them. They were all unanimous in speaking against their abuse.

That evening, after I heard testimony after testimony, I had no choice but to admit to myself that what happened to me, as a child, was wrong. It was illegal and immoral. I had to admit to myself that I was a victim. That all that stuff that happened to me was wrong. I had spent years convincing myself that it was love,

Forgiving Ferns

that it was normal. Lying to myself was easier than facing up to the truth. Now I saw that Denis Byrne was an abuser and that I was the victim and I had no choice.

I spoke to one of the counsellors at the end of the service who invited me to come to the church building the next day to talk things through. So the next day I walked up East Wall in the sunshine. From Rings End to Abbey Street, the whole walk, I was thinking about what had happened to me as a child and how it had affected me.

I arrived and was called into a room where I started to speak vaguely about what had happened. There were awkward moments of silence and shame. Then the counsellor put it to me that I had been abused, raped and wronged. I couldn't take it. I couldn't face the fact that I had been abused.

I had totally convinced myself that Denis Byrne and I were lovers and partners. He had twisted my mind, over those three years, to believe that. It was my coping strategy. It dawned on me that I had been wronged and I started to feel a great loss. My childhood had been stolen. Silence and denial had been my coping mechanism but somehow the councillor seemed to strip those back and I suddenly felt very vulnerable.

I told the counsellor, "No, I am gay. We had a relationship." I was still struggling to admit to myself that I had been robbed. She put it to me that I was not gay. This was not helpful because it felt like, yet again, someone was telling me who I was – was telling me what my sexuality was. I wasn't taking that. I left the counselling and went to the river for a walk.

For weeks after, I wrestled with the fact that I might not be gay and that I was wronged by Denis Byrne. Yet I refused to do anything about it. I started to feel alone and isolated. Because I could not face the truth put to me by the church leaders, they had no way of working with me. They began giving me ultimatums.

I wanted to be involved with church life. I knew you had to live a good life, a clean life. I thought I had no choice over my sexuality. I had convinced myself who I was. I ignored the fact that I enjoyed what I did with Niamh. It seemed that this issue would not go away. I felt very anxious now because, for the third time, I had broken my promise of silence to Denis Byrne. I was paranoid about someone else dying on me.

A few months later I was invited to a Christmas Eve Concert called 'Jesus the healer of broken lives', run by the Fellowship Bible Church.

It was interesting to see so many people at the front talking and sharing about marriage problems and how Jesus set them free from it all.

One man said that it was not until he admitted that he had a problem that he began to get help. I felt the issue of my confused sexuality come up again. It would not leave. In the atmosphere of the music and everyone crying at the meeting, it was haunting me. I had a feeling that someone up there in heaven was trying to tell me something.

The next day was Christmas Day and I didn't have anywhere to go for Christmas. So I went to the church to see what their Christmas service was about. There was an announcement about Jim Hannah, my friend who lived at the Lighthouse on Tara Street. He had been run over by a car and was in intensive care.

My heart sank. I felt terrible. I felt very close and connected with him. He was 19 years old. I went to St James' Hospital, in Donnybrook, and stayed with him as he lay in a coma. He had terrible head injuries.

The whole church was downstairs praying in the waiting room. He lasted two days. On the 27th he was pronounced dead. I felt totally rotten inside. He was buried on the 31st December 1992 in Kilmegan Cemetery, New Castle,

County Down. It plunged me into despair.

I left Dublin and returned home to Gorey. I was full of anger and self-hatred. My whole heart turned against God. Going to funerals brings back all the pain and all the memories of my own parents' funerals. Jim Hannah's tragic death weighed heavy on me.

I remained in a state of numbness and sadness. I found comfort in an old friend and just lived out my time doing the homosexuality thing. If I was a real Christian before Jim's death, I certainly was not one after. I resented God, I hated him, and blamed him for everything.

One day, in a fit of rage, I grabbed a knife when I returned home and stabbed it through my hand. I carved Denis Byrne's name into my forearm. I wrecked my room. I left home for Tara Hill with forty painkillers. As the darkness fell across the Irish countryside, I marched five miles to the top of that hill. I was angry. I hated God. I hated myself. I hated life. I reached the top of the hill and looked out across the freezing cold sea. I looked up at the night sky, at the stars and the moon. I'd often come to the coast to find peace but that night I came to end it all. I took all the pills and I lay down to die. I was so numb I couldn't feel anything. I was desperate and alone.

My left hand was covered in blood from the stab wound. I threw myself on the ground. I lay there waiting for death to come. It wasn't long before exhaustion got the better of me and I passed out from the loss of blood. As I drifted into unconsciousness, I thought, "Excellent. I am free. This is it. I am dying." There, alone on that cold, dark hill, I lay in the grass with the moon as the only witness to my end. Everything was spinning. I felt light-headed and drifted away.

Ouch. A bright light glared into my face. Am I dead? Is it over? The bright light turned out to be the early morning sun. Why am I alive? I turned my head, my neck stiff with lying awkwardly during the night. I brought my hand to my face. It was throbbing with pain. I looked and saw my hand caked in dried blood. I was three miles up a cold mountain. I should have been dead from exposure. I had a major cut on my hand. I had taken up to forty painkillers. Why had I not died?

I felt nauseous and my head felt like someone was driving a bulldozer through it. I looked at the empty tablet container. 'Worming tablets for dogs' the label said.

When I was throwing things around and stabbing myself in a rage the previous day, I obviously picked up the wrong container. I still wanted to die and looked around for a rope or wire or something. As I sat up to look around, a farmer came across the hill and found me sitting there. "What happened to you?" he asked.

"I think I slipped and banged my head," I said.

He took me to Doctor Nixon's surgery. I needed twelve stitches in my hand. The doctor asked me if anything was the matter. He had known my parents and I couldn't tell him. He gave me some painkillers but I felt too sick in the stomach to take them. I went home and suffered the most horrible stomach cramps and diarrhoea.

I had such cramps that I went to the doctor's emergency room at his home. It was there that evening that I told him about the loss of Jim and how I felt about my parents dying but didn't tell him about the suicide attempt. He asked me a few questions like, "Was I suicidal? Had I bought anything unusual from the shops like a new car?" He was checking for any warning signs.

He gave me an injection and told me to go home and rest and go to see him in a few days.

As soon as I got home I collapsed on the bed. I lay there for ages. Dr Nixon had given me valium and I was pretty much 'out of it' for a day or so.

I went to my friend David who I had known virtually all my life. I told him everything. He told me that we had to report this abuse to the priests and let them know what had happened. I wasn't sure that was the thing to do. David was feeling low himself as his partner had left him and returned to London. He also felt very lonely. So we consoled each other.

Chapter 9
Seeking Justice

"Injustice anywhere is a threat to justice everywhere."

Martin Luther King JR (1929 - 1968),

Letter from Birmingham Jail, April 16, 1963.

It was early January 1993, about two weeks after Jim's funeral, and I was feeling pretty desperate and alone. I went to David's house and he said he needed to talk to a priest. I said, "Me too." So we went to see a priest to try and make sense of our lives. I decided in my head that I was going to try and trust the priest to help us. I refused to believe that all priests were like Denis Byrne.

We called at Father William Roberts's home where other priests lived. Father Roberts answered and looked confused and worried He remembered me from the time my parents died. I remember my Mum talking to him and him leaving abruptly.

He said Father McCarthy was on duty, so we

both waited in the corridor for him. I remembered Father McCarthy as I used to be his altar boy. He remembered me and David. He invited us into a room and made us a drink. As he did, Father Roberts had a word in Father McCarthy's ear.

We sat down with Father McCarthy and he had a way of getting to the point without been pushy. So David talked first about his troubles with his lady who had left him. I spoke of the bereavement of Jim Hannah, and how I was confused about sexuality.

I told Father McCarthy the truth about how it started. He suggested that I must have been gay before the 'relationship' with Denis Byrne. But there was no 'relationship' with Denis Byrne according to the counsellor in Dublin. She said it was abuse, rape and manipulation. Father McCarthy disagreed and asked me if I was gay before the relationship with Denis Byrne. As if that made any difference.

He said he was happy to sort it all out for me and help me through the confusion, but I would have to come back when David wasn't with me because my issue would take longer to resolve.

I did meet him on a few occasions. He recorded what had happened to me. He wrote things down and said that it was his duty to inform the Bishop. But he never once condemned what had happened to me. He never once spoke against it. Never once did he say to me that homosexuality was wrong, or that what had happened to me was illegal.

So, for a short period of time, those meetings with Father McCarthy only made things worse. It put the responsibility for the abuse on me. Yet I was hurting, emotionally drained and not strong enough to see what he was doing. He put the protection of the Church above the protection of a child.

Being involved with the Red Cross at many events, I befriended a few policemen and built up some trust with them. One night I was feeling suicidal again and I went to the police station about two o'clock in the morning. I had a cup of tea with Joseph Sullivan, a policeman, and I told him about Denis Byrne. Off the record, he told me that I could make a statement against him, if that made me feel better. But he said it was highly unlikely he would be convicted as he was now in the UK. It would be my word against his. Again I asked myself, who would believe me rather than a priest. No one believed me. No one ever would believe me.

The police didn't care. As far as they were

concerned, I operated a gun smuggling business that they would never be able to prove. My friends, and some of the bikers, were on the wrong side of the law. The police owed me no favours. Despite all the work I did at the Red Cross and all the mountain rescue stuff I took part in, I was still a criminal in their eyes.

I decided I would have one more stab at getting this Denis Byrne problem sorted out. I went to the police sergeant and told him about the abuse. He gave me the same response. So I tried to forget about it and get on with life, as unsatisfactory it was.

I got a job with the local undertaker. I learned a little about embalming and laying out linings in coffins. I went with him on many occasions to collect bodies from homes, taking them to the mortuary. It was a depressing job but, thankfully, it was short-lived.

One of my sexual partners had moved to Birmingham. He invited me to visit him and see what was happening over there, so I agreed.

I travelled over and stayed with him for a few weeks. When I returned to Ireland, I asked my brothers to sell the family home as I was leaving for good and not coming back. My brother Pat was about to get married. My other brother, David, was living with his partner a few miles away. It was time for us all to close this chapter on the house and to move on and go our separate ways.

We put the house on the market and I returned to Birmingham to await the sale of the property. I had mentally run away for years from the abuse. I had mentally run away from facing my sexuality. Now I was running away physically.

I was happy with my decision. I was gay. I was living a gay lifestyle. I let the abuse and the memories of Denis Byrne go. I moved to Birmingham to start my new life. I was convinced I had overcome my demons and left them behind. But you know what? No matter how far you run, you can never run away from yourself.

A few weeks had passed and I was working in Beaufort Park. I was in a strong gay relationship with someone I had known for many years and who I had had sexual relationships with since the age of 15. I felt safe and I trusted him and he trusted me.

I was going to use the money from the sale of the home to train in college to become a nurse or a paramedic or something in the medical field.

It was time to fly back, close the chapter of

Irish life for ever, sign with the solicitors and sell the home, as they had found a buyer. The house was sold for £33,000 Irish pounds. This was split between me and my two brothers.

I had a few thousand stashed away in Ireland from arms sales so I used that to buy a brand-new mobile home for £4,500. It was to be kept on my brother's land as a fail-safe for me.

I left it with my brother for safekeeping. I had a white Toyota van which I used when I was in Ireland to get around. I used to stash some firearms in it and leave it at my brother's new home, parked at the back of his bungalow in Courtown Harbour.

I went to the solicitors and realised that I had made a mistake with my bank accounts. After I withdrew the £4,500 for the mobile home and after I paid off the fees for transporting the mobile home up to my brother's place, I closed all my bank accounts. Meaning that I had to pick up a banker's draft from the solicitors' office. As there was a currency exchange problem, I had no choice but to cash in the £11,000 cheque. I took the cash on the ferry back to Birmingham.

As the ferry crossed the Irish sea, dark clouds stretched out to the horizon, then the sun broke through. Somehow I felt I was leaving the storms of my past behind in Ireland and felt sure there was a brighter future for me in England.

I arrived in Birmingham exhausted from all the change and activity. But now it seemed I was 'home' in a safe place. I had a new start ahead of me and £11,000 in cash in my bag. Things looked good for once. As I sat down and had a coffee after my long journey, my partner asked me if I fancied a kebab. So I gave him some money. He went for the kebab and I lay down on the couch and fell asleep. I slept all night on the couch, washed out from the bus journey and the ferry crossing.

My friend was taking ages. Maybe he had got distracted by someone. I waited the whole day, wondering where he had got to. Then I started panicking, fearing for his safety. Then it dawned on me – No, surely not. – I ran upstairs to check my luggage. Sure enough, he had disappeared with my £11,000. It was one of those moments when you wish, so much, you could rewind time. That horrible feeling of complete betrayal as I knelt on the floor over my open bag, without the money for my new life.

I never saw him again but I promised myself that the next time I saw him, I would kill him. I walked the streets by night and slept by day, not knowing what to do or think. I couldn't cry.

I didn't feel like killing myself. I wanted him to die first.

After thirteen days of rage and confusion, I gave up and went home to Ireland. People looked at me baffled and confused. 'I thought you had sold up and moved away?' they all said. I didn't have the heart to tell my brothers what had happened. I was dumbfounded, shell- shocked and totally drained of energy. So I did what anyone would do. I went to the doctor and again he gave me valium. I went to a friend's house to stay with him for a few days and flaked out on his couch.

Eventually I ended up moving in with him and sleeping with him. I had never known he was gay. I was content that I had somewhere to stay that didn't involve an explanation to my brothers about why things hadn't worked out in Birmingham. But something had changed in me. I started to become angry. Really angry.

Chapter 10

Shooting Foxes

I'd moved in with Stephen and we became partners. I often used to take his shotgun when I went for a walk along the private beach. I would spend days shooting bottles, pigeons, crows, pheasants and rabbits.

I was walking through the fields with his shotgun and I was thinking of Denis Byrne and of Mick, who had stolen my money. I was hurt and angry at the world. I was walking along the side of a ditch when I saw six small fox cubs. They were about three months old.

They were not with their vixen. She was nowhere to be seen. I pointed the single 12-bore shotgun at the chest of one of the cubs and blasted it. I reloaded and repeated this six times until all the cubs were gasping their last breath as they lay dying on the blood-soaked grass.

I felt no pity, no remorse, no guilt. I was thinking, 'This is what I am going to do to you, Denis Byrne. This what I am going to do to you, Mick'.

That same week I had donned a balaclava and embarked on a crime spree to acquire just enough money to get out of Ireland, to try and recoup the lost ground and recover my cash. My aim was to leave Ireland and and begin a new life.

My first major crime, other than importing and selling firearms, was going to be a petrol station. It was situated on the Arklow Road. I went on foot because I knew a little about these sleepy towns' policing policies. I knew their response times. In my first attack on a petrol station, I entered the booth dressed in a boiler suit, balaclava and body warmer, and armed with a knife, baton and a concealed weapon.

I never produced the firearm in the robberies, as that would have been a greater sentence, if caught. Robbery with violence is different to robbery with firearm. The sentence is much stiffer. Being friends with the police and buying mobile homes from them allowed me to pick up information on a few important police matters.

I entered the petrol station and demanded they fill my bag with cash and zip it up. Within seconds of entering the petrol station, I made off with over £450 in cash.

There were to be 19 armed robberies of this nature around the town. Only one of them resulted in anyone getting seriously injured. That was when someone decided to risk his life trying to save insured money that didn't belong to him. He sustained a serious head injury, to my shame.

Throughout this time, I always had help to do the robberies. There was always one of my friends waiting nearby, to drive me from the scene or to come in and help. The police were always looking for one man, never two.

I had planned my last job with an accomplice. We went to the site the following morning – a post office. We knew it would be risky as it was property of the State. Offences against the State usually carry long sentences. But it was the morning that the country folk collect their dole money. So we knew the post office would be loaded with cash.

We drove to the scene, where we were dropped off. We had planned, with the rest of the team, to meet after the robbery about lunchtime in a coffee shop, from where we would travel on the afternoon bus to Dublin. From there we would cross to the UK and start a new life.

We lay low at about 8.30am waiting for the post office to open at nine o'clock. We were in green, army boiler suits, army boots and gloves. We had pickaxe handles with protruding nails, used for maximum intimidation. We had back-up knives and firearms, which we kept concealed.

Psychologically, a pickaxe handle, with about nine ten-inch nails sticking through it, was far more terrifying than the guns we carried.

All our tattoos were covered with plasters. Our eyebrows were coloured with colouring pencils in case we lost the balaclava in a struggle. We were ready to go. We plotted our escape and our route in great detail.

Within seconds of the order to go we both entered the post office. In about one minute we had a bag-load of cash. To our surprise the man who usually worked in the post office was not there. His wife was, and when we went to the other side of the counter we saw a little girl there. She was terrified but we didn't care. We got the cash and made off across the fields.

We were not expecting to hear the noise of racing police cars getting into the countryside so soon. Within about ten minutes we had travelled two miles across the countryside to our destination. Within eight minutes the police were at the scene in this rural town. I was later to find out that the police had a special training day and a strategic meeting about catching me for all the other crimes.

They had drafted in Wexford, Gorey, Enniscorthy and Arklow Garda. Over thirty-five Garda and detectives were hot on our trail.

They had patrols up and down the country roads. They had observations points around the area and neighbours were notified and phoned. The net was closing.

Five miles away from the crime scene we decided it was time to get changed. We thought it was safer to bury the cheques and our clothes and boots in the field. We put the cash, as much as we could, in our pockets. We went to Ballycanew, eight miles outside Gorey on the Wexford Road. We phoned a taxi to come and get us to take us to the town, where we would meet the rest of the crew. We went into Finnegan's pub. We thought we were safe as it was miles away. But there were still police patrols zooming by every few minutes. We thought we'd sit tight and get a taxi later. We thought when we reached Gorey we'd be clear of the police.

After we had ordered a drink, the barman went out of sight. He went to get our drinks but he didn't come back. I got suspicious. I said to my friends that something was wrong. Before we knew it, plain-clothed detectives, armed police and a swarm of police cars swooped on the pub. They pulled us outside and pressed our faces against the wall. They searched us and found the stash of money.

This was the first mistake I had ever made in my criminal career and I was to pay a high price for it. They pushed us into separate police cars and took us to the main police station in Gorey. I got thumped, pressed and scraped against walls and beaten along the way. I did a stupid thing. I head-butted the detective and made his nose bleed and he banged my face into the wall. I was to pay for that during questioning.

I refused to give my name. They already knew my name. My friends at the police station couldn't believe it. They looked on in disbelief as they saw that the man behind all these other robberies was me.

My co-accused asked what he should do. I told him to blame me. To co-operate and get bail. I asked for a towel for my bleeding nose. The detective said, "What?"

I said, "My nose is bleeding. I need a towel."

He said, "Whose fault is that?"

I always loathe sarcasm, so I said to my co-accused friend, "Don't co-operate." My friend did what I said and I got my towel and my phone call. At that point the detectives realised that all they had was a man with a load of cash. So they tried the softly, softly approach.

I phoned the coffee shop and told them to pass on a message to my crew, saying that I was not coming for lunch today. The Garda raced out of the door with some armed police, once they established that I'd phoned the coffee shop instead of my solicitor. But the police were too late. My crew bolted and the firearms were safely back on their way to Belfast. My friend asked me again what he should do. I told him to confess and blame it all on me. I suggested he should try and get bail and I would see him in London.

Whilst my crew was dismantling the operation, they phoned my solicitor on my behalf and they also phoned my brothers and told them what had happened.

I was questioned for hours and beaten at times. Then at 6 pm, after a very tough interrogation, where they tried to get me to admit to some political crimes and kidnapping, which I had nothing to do with, they decided to press charges. I was taken under armed guard in convoy to a special Court in County Wicklow.

The police recommended a remand for me, as I had no fixed address. Actually, this was a lie. I did have a fixed address and they spent the

afternoon searching it. My companion got bail
as planned and I got remanded to Mount Joy
Prison – Europe's toughest prison. The hearing
lasted all of five minutes. I was escorted to a
Wicklow police station, where I was placed in
their custody and transferred to Mount Joy.

It was almost midnight when I got there. I
was hungry and cold and wearing only a track
suit and the rubber slippers they provided. They
searched my clothes for forensic evidence. I was
taken to the registration cells, strip-searched,
showered and then taken to B1 wing. I was
placed in a holding cell with another prisoner
who was in his 60s. I urgently needed some
rest. I'd have to figure this one out in the morning. Bruised and aching all over, and with the
taste of blood still in my mouth, I drifted into a
fitful sleep.

Chapter 11
Captive Thoughts

"And the wild regrets, and the bloody sweats,
none knew so well as I:
for he who lives more lives than one
more deaths than one must die."

Oscar Wilde (1854-1900)

I woke up to the noise of banging doors, rattling keys and strong Dublin accents. Men were shouting on the landings. I thought to myself, "Now what? I've just got to sit here and wait." That afternoon I was moved to a different cell.

I refused to have a longer remand than a week. The judge had the right to remand me for up to three months, so long as we consented, but my brief refused. It meant that at least once a week I would be driven under police escort to the district court. This meant for one day a week I was out of prison, going for a three-hour drive each way and a day in court.

I was allowed more phone calls, on these days, whilst I was in police custody, than when I was in prison detention. Also the food down country was from the local restaurants and it was taken to the police cells for us. So it was better than the food we got at Mount Joy.

At least three times a day I would witness drug-related violence on B1 at Mount Joy. I saw some brutal beatings given and received by officers and inmates. They had this system of settling violence very quickly. Prison violence dictates that, if you're going to injure someone, you must do it quietly and quickly and get at least 200 feet away from the victim before anyone notices.

If a fight broke out on the remand wings, it would be stopped rather quickly, because Mount Joy's way of dealing with violence was to send huge amounts of prison officers in. Large numbers of officers would flood the wings. Safety in numbers. There would be a violent rush of blue uniforms from one end of the wing to the other, which meant they quashed the argument very quickly.

So people got wise to settling arguments. It would take longer for the officers to reach the yard, so a majority of attacks would happen there. For years, people would melt razor blades into the handles of toothbrushes. Bars of soap were put into socks or worse still, batteries into socks for the ultimate weapon.

Violence was brutal and fast. In my time, new wings were being built and cameras installed. Whenever I saw violence, I would just stand and stare. It made no difference to me. I never found it disturbing. I think it was because, inside, I was emotionally numb.

The courts were shutting down for the summer and I had been on remand for almost a month. I was feeling emotionally drained and the suicidal feelings started to return. I just went through a period where I felt responsible for everything I had done wrong. I felt empty inside and dead already.

I got moved to the single-cell units on B1 wing and I was enjoying my space, not having to talk to anyone. I could do a poo in peace instead of having an audience. In Mount Joy you had the old Victorian slopping-out system. Every morning at the 8am unlock, you had to go to the end of the wing and wash out your potty. Humiliating for grown men, but maybe that was the idea.

In the evening you would have to bang on the door to get them to let you out to go to the toilet. I got wise to this and started to bang my door at 7pm and switch on my calling light. It would take at least two hours for the officers to come around and unlock.

One morning I had a visit from my brothers and they were quite unhelpful. They were really disappointed in me because I robbed a post office which was just a few miles away from the village where they lived. I think they were worried about the disappointment and the hurt I caused the neighbourhood.

So when they left the prison, after the visit, I thought I might as well kill myself. I returned to my cell and shut the door. I got a sheet from my bed and I tied one end of it to the end of the bed. I started to twist the sheet in a circular motion. It began to look like a rope. I kept twisting and twisting and before long I had the thinnest, strongest rope made out of sheets.

I hid it under my pillow and waited for the lights to go out. I thought, "Great. At last I am going to die. In a few hours, I will be dead and set free from this life." A few moments after that, the prison door opened. In came three prison officers, announcing a routine prison search. They pulled the blankets off the bed and found the home-made hanging device. They removed me to the hospital wing and made me speak to a doctor.

The following morning, I was transported back to court. I was taken before the judge and there was an agreement that they would remand me and place me under a home order. Meaning, I had to be at home before 8 pm at night. Failure to do so would mean that I would be brought to Mount Joy to await trial rather than be bailed to appear.

I thought this was excellent news. I couldn't believe it. This was my time. I was sure they were loosening their grip on me. 'They are letting me go!' I thought.

I was arrested again a few hours later just for questioning about an alleged kidnapping that the police said I was responsible for. I was questioned for a few hours.

I received more kicking from the police and left the court in the same clothes they gave me – tracksuit and rubber shoes. These two detectives told me that, if I didn't admit to these crimes, they would see to it personally that I got convicted for them regardless. They said that I would receive a very stiff sentence of up to twenty years. Policing has changed a lot since then – tape recorders, video surveillance in cells, etc. But back then it was very basic.

They released me without charge and told me that they would find the evidence that I had done this political kidnapping and that I would be hurting before long. I decided that I was happy to go to prison for stuff I'd done but,

Forgiving Ferns

under no circumstances was I going to go to jail for someone else's wrongdoing.

I thought the court could remand me if I re-appeared. Especially when they heard the seriousness of the kidnap charges. It started to dawn on me that the reason they consented to the temporary release from prison, was so the police could have another stab at interviewing me. I was refusing police interviews while I was in prison. In prison I was the responsibility of the Governor and I could have easily lodged an Article 44 complaint if they tried to interview me while in prison custody.

I was in a catch-22 situation. If I was convicted of all the robberies I had done, I was facing a long time in jail. If I stayed out of prison and they pinned the kidnap charges on me, I was facing an even longer sentence. If I went on the run and they caught me, the sentence would be even longer. Whichever way I looked at it, I would lose. At least if I went on the run there was a chance of getting away.

I booked my passage out of Ireland. I left my homeland with just one set of clothes, a small rucksack and a leather jacket. I dyed my hair blond and wore a pair of clear glasses and a baseball hat. It would be a long time before I returned to Ireland. I boarded as a foot passenger on the Dublin to Hollyhead ferry and arranged to get the coach to London. I was on my way to see Niamh.

Chapter 12

Miracle in Roundwood Park

I arrived at Liverpool Street Coach Station in London in the middle of a heatwave. In contrast to the sleepy villages and towns around Gorey, London was packed with commuters and tourists going to and fro. No one spoke to strangers or greeted anyone here. It was easy to hide in these crowded streets.

I navigated my way across the London Underground to my uncle's house in Shepherds Bush. I arrived at his home and had a cup of tea and drew breath. We chatted about old times.

I got some directions from him about getting to Niamh's address. I didn't know much about the bus routes in London or how to find my way around. Eventually, I managed to find my way to Donnington Court, in Willesden Green.

I arrived at the property, which turned out to be temporary accommodation for people waiting for a council flat. I asked to be let in to visit flat number nineteen. I knocked on the door a couple of times but there was no reply, then looked through the letterbox. The flat was completely bare.

I went down to reception and asked if there was a forwarding address. They said there was but I would have to attend Mahatma Gandhi House in Wembley, if I needed to contact her, because of data protection issues.

I worked out how to get there but I was running out of funds very quickly. I walked for about an hour, all the way to Wembley, until I arrived at the housing association building. I told them that I was Niamh's brother, that I had come with bad news from home and needed to find her. They refused to give me her address and I didn't know what to do next.

So I roamed the sun-baked streets with no place to go. I knew the authorities would track me down if I stayed at my uncle's house. So I pondered how I might get out of this mess.

I was walking through Roundwood Park looking for a place to stay. I even thought I could sleep the night in the park. I lay down on the grass under a tree. It was really hot, even in the shade. I was feeling pretty miserable and had no idea what I was going to do. I had no equipment for a robbery. I had a firearm but that was it. In the UK you need more than firearms. You need local knowledge and a means of escape. You also need three weeks to plan and prepare before doing a robbery. Ireland didn't have a real police force in comparison to the UK. So robbery was not really an option.

I lay down to rest under the tree when I heard some singing in the background. I thought that it must be a circus because behind me was a massive marquee. I thought it strange that they were singing, 'There is a Redeemer'.

I felt drawn towards the tent. They were singing the same songs I used to sing at Riverwalk tearooms. I approached the tent cautiously. I heard the songs and I felt a little emotion running through me. Outside the tent there were several Ford Transit vans, all painted the same. It was the Jesus Army. There were lots of people in fluorescent combat uniforms.

They invited me in and offered me some food from the barbeque – the first meal I had that day. As I ate, they invited me to stay for the service, to listen to the preacher and to the bands. It was fun and, for me, it killed time. I wondered if I could sleep in the tent for the night. I could have some food and then worry about tomorrow in the morning.

They didn't ask any questions about me, no really probing ones any way. I told them my real first name but not my surname. Some of the lads shared the Gospel with me and I started to feel uncomfortable and angry with that. But I thought I should listen to them because they were feeding me.

They asked me if I was homeless and, to a point, I was. They said that they had a farm in Daventry called New Creation Farm. They said it was a rehab centre for the homeless and people with addiction problems. And then the words I was waiting to hear – Would I like to come and live on the Farm?

They said that they had two more days of mission here and then they would be going back to Daventry. I was welcome to go with them. They asked me to help with the stage set -up and they gave me some jobs to do. All the time I was thinking, "What is happening? What am I doing here? This is an interesting turn of events."

The second night there was a preacher called Noel Stanton, the founder of the Jesus Army. He was preaching on forgiveness and love. It wasn't helping me. I felt totally drawn in by this challenging preach and at the end of the meeting he brought out a large dustbin. This black dustbin was an open invitation to every-one there. Noel said, "Take a piece of paper and write down your sin and come up and put it into the dustbin. Leave it with Jesus." The bin was placed at the base of a large cross.

The cross made me recall the abuse. But I thought this was an opportunity to change. How many more chances was I going to get? It seemed a miracle that I'd ended up here instead of being homeless. I made a commitment to try and follow God. I walked up to the bin, took out my firearm and slipped it into the bin.

This was the first major step I took and it felt significant. God had disarmed me and now he could begin his work in me. The moment I made the decision to lay the firearm down, I felt a release.

People came and prayed for me. They stood around me and laid their hands on my shoulders. Suddenly, God seemed very close to me, touching me deep inside, and I fell to the floor. I felt the power of God flow through me. This had never happened to me before. I felt peace, love, warmth and acceptance. Something was happening to me. Something real. What a miracle! I had been rescued from being homeless and on the run.

But God had only just started with me. I went back to Daventry with the Jesus Army guys and spent almost four months with them on New Creation Farm. I was getting prayed for and falling down quite often. I was also getting involved with Christian community life. It felt great. At least there was a roof over my head and I had some friends, a place to stay and food to eat. For me it was a respite but I soon got restless.

Four months later I asked the leaders if I could be transferred to the Battle Centre based in Ealing. I wanted to return to London in the hope that I might find Niamh. I had recovered my strength and wanted to get back to my original plan.

The Jesus Army have centres all over Europe. I thought if I could convince them that I'd be better working in London with homeless people, then they would let me go to one of their other centres. I had no drug problems and no alcohol problems. The only problem that was raising its ugly head was homosexuality.

Eventually they agreed and moved me to the Battle Centre. There were about thirty people living in two very large houses, side by side, in Ealing. It was good to be back in the city with people my own age. I had a better circle of friends in the Battle Centre and there was less control because it wasn't a rehab centre.

We got involved in large-scale outreach events and it was fun. But I decided that I was going to try and deal with my homosexuality problems. My mind was changing and looking at homosexuality differently. Perhaps it was because I was responding to the structure and clean living of the Jesus Army.

In my heart, I wanted to make an effort to get this confusion dealt with. It was easy not having a girlfriend in the Jesus Army because a large number of them were radical celibates. There was never any pressure to find a girlfriend or get married. But there was pressure to remain celibate.

I began to talk about the abuse to the pastors and started to tell them my story. They challenged me to push out the darkness of homosexuality. I told them about the crimes, which may have been a bit naïve. They told me that they would never shop me to the police but challenged me to give myself up. They gave me an ultimatum. I was to give myself up to the police and go to prison and reach prisoners with the Gospel. I told them I couldn't do it. Sadly, they made me leave the Battle Centre and the Jesus Army.

I felt betrayed again for being honest. I had told the Church in Ireland about my abuse and they covered things up. I told the Fellowship Bible church about the struggles with sexual sin and homosexuality and they kicked me out. Then I told the Jesus Army that I had unresolved issues with the police and that I couldn't deal with it and they rejected me.

I walked the streets of London thinking it was time to turn myself in. I went to Wembley High Street and looked for a police station. On the border of Alperton Sudbury and Wembley, I found a police station. I rang the police station in Ireland, back in Gorey, and asked them what would happen to me if I gave myself up.

They told me that I would probably still get twenty years minimum but they would take into consideration that I'd turned myself in. I felt vulnerable and not strong enough to rough it on the streets of London, but that is what I was facing. I had to find somewhere to stay, be homeless or be in prison.

I went into the police station but there was a queue. So I waited in the queue, wondering what would happen. I approached the desk with every intention of turning myself in.

The policeman opened the shutter to serve me and said, "Yes?" I looked him in the eye. There was a long pause. I wanted to open my mouth but fear gripped me. I asked him for directions to Wembley. He gave me directions and I left the police station. I went outside with a sigh of relief. I made a decision. I thought, 'Stuff it, if I have to be homeless I will be homeless, but I am not going to prison for something I didn't do.'

I walked down Wembley High Street and, incredibly, within a few minutes, members of the London Church of Christ met me on the street and started talking to me. They asked me if I was interested in going to a Bible study with them. I agreed and a moment later they told me about the homeless project they had. By 10pm that night I was in a flat with three other members of the London Church of Christ. God had given me a miracle and kept me from homelessness for a second time.

Chapter 13
Meeting Claire

Once I was safely bedded down in a flat with the London Church of Christ, I soon realised that there was a vast difference between this church and the Jesus Army. The Jesus Army asked fewer questions, were more accepting and allowed you freedom to talk about your past hurts when you were ready.

I was quickly whisked off to meet the leader of the Harrow and Brent Sector of the London Church of Christ. I was taken to his house for coffee. I made things up as they quizzed me intensely – Who was I? Where was I from? How did I end up homeless? I told them some truth mixed with half-truths.

Eventually I realised they were being polite by showing me that they were interested in me as a person. But, in fact, behind the smoke-screen of nice, probing questions lay an ulterior motive. It wasn't enough for them that I believed in Jesus or that in 1992 I had been baptised with the Fellowship Bible Church in Dublin.

Over a period of two days I received the five teachings of induction into the London Church of Christ. I was encouraged to be baptised by them. I thought, if I don't accept their teaching, they will remove me. So I went along with it. They helped me find a job. I called in a favour from someone I knew from my former life and acquired new identity papers. Then I thought it was time to get out of this cult.

I'm sure the London Church of Christ is nothing short of a religious sect, a controlling cult. They even arrange people's marriages. Every Saturday night, they would insist that I take a sister out for a meal on a date and to do this until I found the one for me.

I was totally uncomfortable with this and I began to look for a way out. I was with the London Church of Christ for three months. Three months of almost being brainwashed. I had to hand a lot of my wages over to them on Wednesday evenings and Sunday afternoons.

One Sunday afternoon I was with another member of the L.C.C. We stood on Kingsbury High Street in North West London. We were trying to invite people to church. I went into McDonald's where I met some other brothers chatting to some people they had managed to talk into going to the service.

I met this Nigerian man – his name was Robert or Bob. We spoke over a Big Mac, talking about the L.C.C. I could see that he was a genuine believer. I could see that he was interested in this fellowship and looking to become a member of it. It seemed to be much more organised than other churches he had attended.

Over a period of two months we became friends and eventually he invited me to his church. It was Woodcroft Evangelical Church. I met some people there. It felt a little dull to be honest, but it didn't have a controlling influence like the L.C.C. or the Jesus Army.

I met the pastor who happened to be Irish. He was from East Belfast, a proper Protestant. I couldn't see past his background any more than he could see past mine. But we did talk and I left after the service and went back to L.C.C.

Deep down in my spirit I quite liked the service. I thought I'd return there. Of course, when I spoke to the London Church of Christ about my visit, they hit the roof. They said I was 'in sin' and that I needed to be baptised.

They didn't see the Evangelical Church as a Christian church. I didn't like the control. I didn't like them making derogatory comments about the pastor of Woodcroft, in spite of him being a Protestant. So I was drawn back to the fellowship and I met with the pastor again and outlined the situation with the L.C.C. I told him that I had no other place to stay and that I hadn't got enough money together to get my own place.

The pastor, Paul Sands, spoke with Bob and before long I was invited to stay with Bob in Colindale and I attended his church. On a few occasions the London Church of Christ tried to persuade me to go back, by turning up at Bob's house and trying emotional blackmail.

But Pastor Sands put me right on biblical teachings. I realised that this London Church of Christ was wrong, all wrong. In Woodcroft I had freedom. I argued with Paul over many political problems and many spiritual problems were thrashed out.

I started to trust him – he felt safe to be around, in spite of his strong will and sometimes abrasive nature, that accompanies any Irishman. He had a pastoral heart. I could feel the care and his genuine faith.

A few months passed and I decided that I was going to commit to this church to try and rebuild my life. It was a matter of a few months before I would realise that this was where I belonged. This was what I truly believed. This was where I could begin again to find myself. I felt loved, cared for and safe. I felt needed and involved.

Bob and I had a keen interest in martial arts and we had some great times sparring in his living room, I taught him some techniques I knew and we went to a club. It was a healthy friendship and I had a lot to thank him for.

I could have a friendship with a bloke where sex was not part of it. I could talk to him and not feel threatened. Sometimes I used to get wound up by him because we would go to church together. But he had African timing – he was always leaving for church when he should have been arriving.

We arrived in church one Sunday morning and I was introduced to some friends of Bob that I'd never met before. I met this young, fresh lady called Claire and some other people. But Claire was the name I remembered because it was an Irish name. She was English but I liked her. She seemed genuine and intelligent.

The following weekend I met with Bob to go to a party. It turned out that Claire was there as well. We didn't speak much. I couldn't speak to her because I wasn't very confident with women.

The next day I had an appointment at the dentist. When my time came, I went through and sat in the chair. To my great surprise, the dental nurse was Claire. I couldn't believe it.

As time passed by we kept bumping into each other. I wasn't interested in a relationship, nor was I looking for one – I could barely take care of myself. But I was interested in companionship and I felt with Claire there was something there. I was a gay criminal wanted on terrorist charges, hanging out with an English woman whose Dad happened to be a tailor for the Queen.

What fun we had the night I first met Claire's Mum and Dad. They had this great gift of hospitality. They would often have people back for tea or supper and, on Sundays, for lunch.

Claire invited me for lunch at her place with some others on the Sunday, so I agreed to go. While I was there, I went straight to their fridge and made myself a sandwich and a cup of tea. This sort of behaviour was common in Ireland but it was something Claire's parents hadn't seen before. They probably felt like they were being invaded.

I remember feeling homesick. I had not sat down to a family meal like this since I was fifteen and here I was seven years later, sitting down at a family meal. It felt special and yet difficult also. I had become accustomed to my own way of life and didn't know what to do or say. I starting eating the food before they said grace. And then the questions started. I tried to be as honest as possible. I told them about my parents dying, that they died about ten days apart and that I had come to England to get away from it. Which was sort of the truth.

I liked being at their house. That afternoon me and Claire – snogged. It was weird. I was showing sexual interest in a woman. It was something I thought impossible after Niamh. It felt both weird and wonderful. I felt cared for and I felt loved. I started to fall in love with the idea of living again.

I really began to feel that God was starting to turn my life around. I really felt part of this community of Christian believers. And with my new girlfriend things just seemed fantastic. I began to feel fulfilled by life. But always at the back of my mind was the nagging question – what if Claire finds out about my past?

Most days, my shady past seemed to be dissolving away. Claire and I became soul mates. I embraced my new lifestyle and my new faith and friends. It was like the family and the home I never had. I secretly hoped my past would stay buried.

Chapter 14
Drumming up Support

Tony, my friend from church, saw that I had an interest in the music group and ministry, so he invited me to attend a new Christian group that was forming, called Psalm Drummers. We were very into Soul Survivor and Delirious, and I felt that the music helped me release things. It was positive and fun.

Psalm Drummers met the first Monday of every month at Holy Trinity Church, Brompton. Here I was to find friends, a purpose and a gifting I never knew I had. I attended regularly and met people like Callum Reese, drummer for Vineyard, Mike Sturgis, Phil Crabbe, Graham Kendrick, and Martin Neil, drummer and musicologist who played with Kevin Prosh and the Black Peppercorns. I felt honoured to be sitting at the feet of these world-class drummers and percussionists. These guys played with the world's greatest. Callum Reese's Dad drummed for AC-DC and it was amazing that they were talking to me like I was their buddy.

Terl Bryant, the founder of Psalm Drummers, spoke openly about the importance of vision, seeing visions and declaring the presence and the coming of the Lord through drumming. It struck a beat in my heart. I remembered the drummers of my town and how they were used to declare the arrival of the Eucharist. In Belfast drumming was used to provoke. Here in this place, drumming was being used to declare the greatness of our God. It was used as a mighty tool to bring change, to bring the denominations together and to break down strongholds across churches. It was a calling and a vision I bought into and it was to be an integral part of my deliverance.

Terl Bryant was the instrument in my life that changed the rhythm of my heart. Just spending time with him, watching him and learning from him helped me no end. Here was one of the greatest Christian drummers and percussionists in all Europe and he was befriending me. He saw my heart's desire to give back to the Lord an offering of thanks and gratitude. To serve him and to thank God for the times my suicides failed, for the times my life had been falling apart yet God had rescued me from homelessness. He helped me put my true feelings into rhythm and I was marching to a new beat.

I communicated with the Lord on a new level. Before long I was playing my drums with them in places I had never known before. I played in St Paul's Cathedral, Wembley Stadium, Reading Stadium and Berlin Stadium. We played before a million viewers on Songs of Praise from Stonleigh. Before long I was to become a group leader of Psalm Drummers. It just got better and better. Psalm Drummers rapidly became the fastest-growing Christian Drummers family, spanning the globe. And my love for drumming and my love for God grew greater. I asked the Lord one day to change me and change me for ever. I told the Lord this was my heart's desire, to serve him through music and drumming. I told the Lord I couldn't do it unless he set me free from my past – I was still struggling with homosexuality. No amount of prayer or teaching or counselling was working.

In my heart, I desired to be true and transparent. I wanted to be intimate with Claire without the distractions of same-sex temptation. I wanted to be truthful about who I was. I wanted to be free.

In reality I was still on the run from the police. But I longed to be me again.

Chapter 15
The Fear of Rejection

Fear, when it gets a grip, will control us and cause us to make bad decisions. I wanted to tell Claire the truth. Every time I thought about doing so, memories of telling my father the truth came flooding back. I told him the truth and he died. I told my Mum the truth and she died. Bad stuff always seemed to follow whenever I told anyone the truth about my past. This fear was the main reason why I couldn't tell Claire the truth about my sexuality or my criminal past.

I told lie after lie in order to create an imaginary history, so I could be someone other than a gay criminal with warrants for my arrest. Looking back, it probably would have been better to tell Claire and let her have the option of knowing the real me. But everyone I'd told in the past had rejected me or condemned me. I suppose I should have given Claire more credit – she deserved to know the truth. And with hindsight, I don't think she would have rejected me. I would have been challenged to work through my past but that wouldn't have been a bad thing.

The whole situation began to weigh very heavy on me. I was now working in a rehabilitation centre for mental health and had completed my NVQ in mental nursing. Claire and I were about to be married. I was constantly worried that any day now I was going to be exposed for what I really was. I often thought of running away from the situation because I didn't feel that my relationship would survive the truth.

I really thought I couldn't marry her. I was wanted by the police. I could marry her but one day they could break down the door and Claire and I would be finished anyway. I felt there was absolutely no one I could talk to about it. I loved her and that was certain. I just didn't think I could trust anyone. The fear of rejection kept me from sharing with Claire what had gone wrong in my life. I was a prisoner of my own secrets.

Days before our wedding, I remember going to counselling in an attempt to try and discuss a little about my past. It was just too painful. I couldn't comprehend what had happened myself. So it was impossible to share about it with others. So I decided that I must grit my teeth, get married and get busy making a life – or bring my life to an end. Yes, the suicidal thoughts were never far away.

The morning of my wedding I was so stressed with the fear of letting Claire down, I threw up. She deserved much better than me. She deserved to be happy. I had started to care for someone like never before. I had started to like people again. I was interested in people and interested in being part of a group. I thought of how I had been so very alone when I went to look for Niamh. That's how it would be if I ran now. I was in constant turmoil.

Then, of course, there were all the wedding arrangements. There was no way I could back out now, not after thousands of pounds had been spent on wedding cakes, dresses, receptions and honeymoons. I had to go ahead with this.

Claire and I wanted to be together. She deserved her moment of happiness. I think I would have killed myself if I had run out and caused her that hurt and pain. It was my love for Claire that made me stay. Some may say that if I had loved her, I would have told the truth. But in my mind, I thought the truth was best kept to me. What she didn't know couldn't hurt her. How wrong I was.

After the wedding, I was involved in the outreach team at the Woodcroft Evangelical Church. I felt as free as a bird in marriage. I was very happy and content. Yet at the back of my mind was always the fear of the police coming to the house. But Claire and I were happy together and we started to plan a family.

One day, I came home in a brand new Ford Mondeo. I was parking outside a friend's house, to pick up church keys, when a man approached me with a knife and told me to give him the car keys. I gave him the car keys but he still insisted he wanted to stab me. As he lunged in front of me with the knife, trying to stab me in the neck, I reacted as I would have done in my criminal days. I grabbed his wrist and turned it completely around. He made a gut-wrenching noise as both his radius and ulna snapped in half as I disarmed him. I was trained in control and restraint techniques. In the heat of the moment, I virtually ripped his arm out of the socket and he almost passed out with the pain. He still managed to run away and leave the scene. But his arm was broken in three different places. I reckoned he would be caught as soon as he checked into the hospital. So although I was a Christian, I still had the instinct to retaliate. My demons were coming to the surface again and I was reminded of my past.

I decided not to pursue the robber but instead phoned the police. They attended the scene and

took the attacker's knife to check for fingerprints. As the days past while they checked the
prints, I was thinking it was only a matter of
time before they realised that those fingerprints
on the knife were mine.

I was more concerned, though, with my reac-
tion to the attack. I had damaged this man's arm
without a second thought. I realised I was still
hardened on the inside. Why hadn't Christianity changed me to the point of making me care
for people? I went home and told Claire what
had happened and I ended up in the newspaper
– 'Martial Arts Man Breaks Attacker's Arm'.

The next two years were relatively unevent-
ful. I was progressing with my training in mental health nursing. I was working in a residen-
tial home for the elderly in Hendon. Claire and
I had just moved to a smaller flat opposite our
church. I was really trying to become a better
Christian and a better person. I was working
hard and I believed I had a relationship with the
Lord and I believed it to be a real one.

Claire came home one day and told me she
was pregnant. Wow! I thought it was wonderful. It was the vote of confidence from God I
needed. He had shown me more trust by blessing us with a baby.

About nine weeks into the pregnancy Claire

miscarried and lost the baby. It was a very sad time; loads of people came to visit us and to pray with us. I felt pushed aside as many men do when their wives miscarry. Many people assume that it is just the woman who is hurting. How wrong they are.

In the following months our church was celebrating it's seventieth anniversary. Chris Bowater, an international worship leader and teacher, was a regular attender at our church. He was leading the worship and called Claire out to the front. Claire was always holding a baby belonging to someone. It was Claire's birthday, so he wished her a happy birthday. He was trying to use Claire holding a baby as an illustration of how God holds us. Claire became emotional and upset. So I went to the front of the church to stand with her. Chris is known for his prophetic gifting. Chris, without any prior knowledge of our miscarriage, opened his mouth and began to speak into our lives. He told Claire, "You will be reunited with that little one." The church who knew we'd suffered a miscarriage was taken aback; many people became emotional, as we did. He told us that God was going to restore to us 'the years which the locusts have eaten'. He said some very special things to us that night and it sort of released us from the pain and hurt of the miscarriage.

Chris called me to the front of the meeting and said, "Young man, there is a season of tears coming. There is coming a time for three months. You will weep and sow in tears and reap in joy." He said to me that the Lord had laid on my heart, the heart of both a lion and a lamb. That I had the heart of a lamb to love the lost. And the heart of a lion to roar at injustice. He told me that I had suffered many miscarriages (not necessarily speaking of losing a baby) but I had been robbed of many things. He could see that in me.

It was that night I realised something in me had changed for ever. I was not just being encouraged by my Christian family. But God was giving me a personal message in front of five hundred people. I felt I had completely side-tracked the service. But now I realise this is the family of God. Here we can be real. There was no more fear of rejection – it disappeared. I felt closer to God than I had ever felt. In my spirit I felt all my worries and my fears were going to be over soon. I felt encouraged. I felt some release. I felt great. But I was very concerned about what he meant by 'a season of tears'. It was to make sense to me quicker than I anticipated.

Chapter 16

A Season of Tears

It wasn't very long after the evening that Chris Bowater prophesied over our lives. I was busy with Psalm Drummers and busy with church and with work. We discovered Claire was pregnant. I was excited and optimistic about this. Then we went for the scans and all seemed well, so we were very hopeful. The summer was coming and Claire was to be pregnant in the summer. But we didn't care. She was having a great pregnancy.

As usual, I woke up at 6.30am to drive to work at Hendon. Just the day before, I had received confirmation of a nursing post in the brain injury rehabilitation unit at Napsbury Hospital. I'd attended interviews there and was successful, securing the post. I was finally working back in rehabilitation. I was very happy about that.

I arrived at the elderly mental health unit in Hendon. It was chaos – the fire alarm had been set off by a resident there and it was getting a little out of hand, as the residents were getting stressed with the noise of the alarm. I walked into the unit to be faced with a load of firemen. So I gave them the keys to deactivate the alarm. At this point, one of the residents had a massive epileptic seizure – the start to another typical day. In the middle of the chaotic scene, the phone rang. I told one of my care assistants to answer it. They came back and told me to come upstairs. Claire needed me urgently. I took the phone and Claire said that there were armed police at the house asking for me. I said, "Tell them I will be right there."

My mind racing, I drove home to try and manage the situation. Along the Hendon Road I thought to myself – do I stay or do I go on the run again? I felt the Lord telling me to stay calm and to trust him. I screamed at the top of my voice, "OK! I trust you!"

I went home as fast as I could, only to find that the police and the helicopters had left. Claire said that they had raced off to my workplace.

"What's this about?" Claire asked through tears. I paused and looked shocked. I was not trying to hide anything any more. It was time for the truth. Claire was three months pregnant. I began to stutter and stammer an answer, but where would I begin? I was interrupted by the phone ringing. Claire answered it. It was PC Gordon Sawyer, a friend of ours. Claire put him onto me. He asked me if I knew why they wanted me.

"Yes," I said. "I will wait here at the house. Don't worry, I am not going on the run again. But please," I said, "don't storm the house. I am not armed and Claire is here with me. Take it easy when you get here."

The delay would give me a chance to explain things to Claire.

Claire and I had a few minutes. She said, "I don't care what you've done, you're my husband and I am sticking by you, no matter what." I looked at her thinking, "You deserve an explanation." But I wasn't given the time.

The police arrived with guns and dogs. They entered the property and said they were from New Scotland Yard's organised crime unit. They searched me, calling me by my real name. They told me that they were taking me to Colindale Police Station for temporary detention, to await a slot at Hendon Magistrates. I was to await a hearing concerning an extradition warrant. I was taken away in handcuffs under armed guard to Colindale Police Station. Gordon booked me in and came into my cell. I explained to him what had happened. He said he was going back to

Claire to see if she was ok and would keep her informed.

As he turned to go I called him back. I told him if he hadn't been here for this arrest, I would have probably shot my way out. I asked him, if I surrendered my firearms from my house, would I be prosecuted for possession of them? He said, "Firearms offences are the least of your worries."

He went back to Claire and the firearms were removed. I still don't know what happened to them to this day. Gordon returned and gave me a Gideon's New Testament. I took it from him and I remained in the cell until they came and got me, photographed me and fingerprinted me. I think they had tracked me down from the guy who robbed me. They ran the fingerprints that they retrieved from his knife through the system. I was shuttled into the detention centre beneath the post office next to Hendon Magistrates. I met a lawyer for all of two minutes through the door. I was anxious and I thought of my poor wife. Claire what have I done? Why didn't I tell her? What a way to find out. I thought I was going to lose her for sure. I would never see my child being born. I would return to Ireland and spend the rest of my days in prison.

Yet through all the chaos and fear, somewhere in my spirit I heard a small voice. "Trust me. Trust me. Trust me." It was all I could hear. I opened the New Testament trying to settle my mind and read, 'Mercy triumphs over judgement.' I began to think that I didn't want to fight extradition. I could fight it and wait in prison for five years. No. Let's go home. Let's agree with the extradition. Let's get out of here. Let's face the music. My attitude and demeanour had changed. I really cared for Claire. I cared that I had hurt her, cared that I was about to lose her.

I was marched up to the dock of Hendon Magistrates, where I spoke to confirm my name. I almost turned my back on the judge. We were trained not to acknowledge UK judges, but to claim political status. Instead, I decided to consent to the extradition. I looked across the courtroom and there was Claire with her Mum and Dad, Paul Sands the Pastor, Darren Chubb and PC Gordon Sawyer. The detective gave his evidence in inaudible whispers out of respect for me, at the request of Gary, so that Claire would hear the full story from me and not rattled off clinically in court. The judge remanded me to Wormwood Scrubs to be extradited under the Offences Against the State Act and the Extradition and Terrorist Act. I was to be put in the custody of the Garda Siochana at a date yet to be determined. I was taken under escort straight to Wormwood Scrubs, where I awaited extradition.

I began to feel relieved that I was no longer on the run from the police. But I deeply regretted causing so much disappointment and pain to my new-found family. I had been married to Claire for two years when this happened and she was three months pregnant. Claire's Mum and Paul Sands and Clarie's mum wrote me a little note saying they were with me, that they supported me. Yes, they were disappointed and hurt, but they wrote that they were standing by me. Claire also wrote a note to me saying that she would stand by me for ever. Pastor Sands also wrote a note to me saying, 'There is now no condemnation for those who are in Christ Jesus.' And he didn't condemn me either. I felt relieved yet concerned. Unlike the last time I was arrested, I felt emotional pain, yet I felt a lot more positive about it. There seemed to be light at the end of the tunnel. After getting to Wormwood Scrubs I lost my appetite because of the number of cockroaches running around. It was hot and very clammy. I was locked up for twenty-three and a half hours a day. I was brought to an overnight holding cell because I was a political prisoner – no national extradition case was allowed to mix with the other prisoners.

I was only allowed one visit in the time before my extradition. Claire and Paul Sands came to visit me. They had to be searched, as did I. There would be no physical contact. We were given one hour. I had one hour to get Claire to stay with me. One hour to convince her I still loved her. One hour to apologise. One hour to explain. It wasn't enough because all I got was: Who was I? What was my real name? Why was I being extradited? How many shooting murders was I involved in? Was I part of the IRA? Was I going to be killed if I returned home?

I chose not to answer any of those questions. Instead, I just reassured Claire and Paul that I loved Claire and I was sincere about most things. I was reassured that they were going to stick by me. Paul Sands had connections in Dublin. He used them to find me a barrister and brief. I spent five days in Wormwood Scrubs, writing letter after letter to Claire, telling her I was sorry. Then the day came. I was allowed one phone call. I was transferred to Heathrow police station to be extradited out of RAF Northolt that night. But they lied to me – I was not to be flown home until the next morning and from a different airport. The security measures were tight.

Pastor Sands and Claire came to Heathrow Station and waited hours to see me, only to be denied a visit. It was 11 pm and they still were not allowed see me. Pastor Sands argued with the police. But the police refused a visit from a pregnant wife, whose husband was being flown out of the country to face his fate. I wasn't allowed to see her, let alone hold her.

The next morning I could hear a lot of Irish accents outside the police cell. The Garda Siochana had moved in to come and get me. The custody sergeant apologised to me for not allowing me a visit from Claire. He said it was because they were overstretched, but his efforts to appease me were in vain. I reached over the desk and told him, "One day soon you will pay for that!" The twenty-year-old custody police officer went pale, as members of the An Garda mocked the rookie cop, saying, "Ahh! The General has passed judgement on you, now you're stuffed." That young policeman didn't know who he was dealing with. I am sure these days he treats all his prisoners with a little more respect. I put the fear of God into him even though I was only messing with him.

I said to the An Garda, in my own language, "Conas a Ta Tu (How are you?). It's been a long time, Sergeant O Reardon."

He said, "We've got you now, haven't we?"

I knew the Garda very well indeed. We had a history and learned to respect each other. I knew they weren't going to rough me up like his colleagues would. The men that came to take me home were people who had lived and worked in the town of Gorey since before I was born. We had a rapport. We talked as we boarded the plane. We flew out and I thought I might never see Claire again, despite all her reassurances, despite all the nice words. The reality was that I'd had it now. Yet, in my spirit, I had a feeling that it was going to be OK.

When I arrived back in Ireland, for the first time in almost eight years on the run from the police, I was taken to the Bride Well in Dublin, where I was charged with nineteen armed robberies and a string of firearms offences. I was remanded to wait for B1 wing of Mount Joy Prison. I had returned to the very cell where I thought I was going to hang myself eight years previously. Only this time I knew something was different. The prison had changed. It was overcrowded, full of violence and rife with drugs. Attacks on people were constant. Yet this time, when I looked at the violence, it churned my stomach. It affected me. It was not like before. Something in my heart had changed.

Something in my spirit was different. Those things which never bothered me before were troubling me now. It was like I had lost my defences. God, good relationships with people and the love of Claire had made me soft inside. I was no longer the angry man who was out of touch with his feelings. But the heart of the lion and compassion and love for Claire and others was there. The heart of the Lion that was to roar at injustice was there also. I spent three months in Mount Joy prison awaiting my trial. Just as Chris Bowater had prophesied, it was a season of tears.

Chapter 17

Mercy Triumphs over Judgement

Many people flew over from the UK. People from Woodcroft Church stood beside me and visited me. People knew from Claire the struggles I had come through in life. People saw my potential and they had grace for me. They did not condone what I had done. They had a simple choice: to accept me or reject me. I wasn't really asking anyone for favours or looking for support. I felt that I didn't deserve any support.

Claire, her parents and my brother Pat came for a family visit. I had one hour with them. It was good to see Claire looking better than she did the morning of my arrest. She had a big bump – our baby. The prospect of missing the birth was grating on me but I was trusting that God would do a miracle. There seemed to be no way to get out of this mess, other than do my sentence, or simply die. Dying was not an option – I finally had something to live for. The prospect of a real life had changed my whole perception.

Claire's Mum and Dad showed me support and love. I had them on my side and it made the world of difference. In a world where parents are usually defensive and protective of their own children, Claire's parents saw beyond immediate circumstances. They didn't judge me but accepted me. And they trusted God, as I did, that mercy would triumph over judgement. We spoke in the glass booth and Claire's Mum seemed to believe that I was coming home with them that week.

It was a few days before my trial when my barristers and legal team came to tell me some news. In Hendon Court, Sergeant Bullimore was asked by the judge what charges I had been extradited on. The detective showed that he had one warrant for the post office robbery. The post office robbery, which was an offence against the State, carried a maximum penalty of fourteen years. The legal team told me that my co-accused was sentenced to seven years. So, for that, we were looking for up to fourteen years because I had chosen to abscond.

The judge consented to the extradition for the post office robbery but was not consulted about the fact that I was being charged with other firearms offences and robbery charges. These other nineteen charges were kept from the court in the UK. The judge asked if I was wanted for any other charges in the Republic of Ireland. The extradition team said no. Therefore I consented to the extradition. If I had known that I was being extradited on other charges, I could have objected to the extradition and fought it. So the Irish government lied to the British Government and this issue was becoming a political one. The Irish police force might have perjured themselves in a British court.

My legal team told me that I could only be charged with what I was extradited for. I asked if that meant when I served my sentence I could be charged with all the other crimes? They said, 'No'. They told me that the Irish police couldn't hold charges back from the court and, because they lied in the British court, the extradition would be unlawful. I could only ever be charged with this one post office robbery. All the other charges had to be struck out.

I was still looking at being jailed for fourteen years. But my lawyers said that with my past, losing my parents and being suicidal, they could try and mitigate it. So I agreed to go forward on a plea of guilty and to offer compensation to the victims.

The next morning I woke up with a degree of optimism. I had a suit delivered to the prison.

I woke up and had breakfast at 6am. I had a shower and got ready for my trial. I went to ask about getting my personal belongings and my wedding ring before I went to court. They said that I was not to bother. The property department would look after them. After all, I would be coming back. They refused to allow me to get my personal belongings and they escorted me in chains to Wexford Circuit Court.

We entered in by the back door. There were a lot of media people outside. I was marched into court and I had to wait in the court for a number of hours before it was our turn. We had a meeting with the solicitors and they told Pastor Paul Sands that there was no hope of me coming home. Pastor Sands said, "He is coming home today with me." I wished I'd shared his optimism.

The case was called at 5pm. I sat in chains all day in court waiting, and various people were called – Pastor Sands included. The prosecutors tried hard to discredit him. They asked many questions about my character and tried to discredit his replies. They tried to show the court that because of all the lies I had told, I was not a changed man.

MI5 intelligence reports showed me attending church groups and praise parties. They showed that I was taking part in community projects and holding down a job. Nothing in the reports suggested that I was politically involved. The court was shown that I was rehabilitated and that the crime was one of desperation. The other crimes were kept from view of the judge and they couldn't be presented in court for fear that the Irish government would face awkward questions about why they had lied in a British court.

Then the judge asked some questions about Claire being pregnant and they asked me to take the stand. I was released from the chains and the cuffs. I presented my case and my background and what I had achieved since I had been in the UK. The judge accepted the accounts given. But the judge asked about my co-accused who was sentenced to seven years. The defence argued that they had no knowledge of his past. The judge decided that she would give me the same sentence as he had received for the crime but, on the condition that I kept out of trouble for three years, she would suspend the sentence.

I walked out of court trying to catch my breath. Everyone was shell-shocked and dumbfounded. The solicitors asked me what happened. The police followed me outside, gave me a pat on the back and said, "Well done." My barristers thought that I had been sentenced but my other solicitor said, "No, he's been released! He is free!"

They couldn't believe it. I was a free man. There were hugs and kisses, jumping up and down, up and down! Three months in prison – a season of tears. Now I was released with only a suspended sentence. That evening, I was safe in Claire's arms, soon to be heading back to the UK where our baby would be born. It seemed like a dream.

Two weeks later I attended my work place, explained what had happened and told them the truth. The brain injury management had a meeting. They decided to give me my job back. I received many miracles in that season. Once again, mercy triumphed over judgement!

Chapter 18
Moving to Suffolk

Settling back into the routine and rebuilding relationships with people wasn't easy at first. After all, I had broken trust. I had lied my socks off in an attempt to hide my past from people. Fear of rejection was one of the things I was wrestling with. I kept my head down and I became the father of a lovely little daughter, who we called Stephanie. It was fun being a dad and quite a privilege. Life continued and I started to get more and more heavily involved with Psalm Drummers. I could safely say that I was being changed. Old hurts, fears and anger were falling off me. It seemed that God was stripping back the past – peeling back the layers of pain. Slowly, as I met with the drummers and prayed and played, strongholds started to fall away, revealing issue after issue.

Then one day my brother phoned me and told me that Father Denis Byrne was dead. He told me that he had died of HIV and it was rumoured all over the town that he had been sentenced for crimes in Liverpool. He had been removed from Christ the King Church where he was a priest, got involved in a gay relationship, had contracted HIV and subsequently died. God had given me justice, I felt that very strongly. I was sad in one part because it seemed that no one would ever know for sure of his guilt or his crimes. But in due course all that was to change.

Two years had passed since my extradition and release. We were still enjoying the church and relationships were restored. Since we had a second baby on the way, we believed it was important to try and get on the property ladder. Our rented apartment was clearly not big enough. We were praying and seeking God to advise us and to help us buy a home. We were discouraged by house prices in London. Claire had stopped working as a dental nurse, and three and half times my salary was all they would give us. So we decided to look for cheaper property. We looked at Cambridgshire, Bedfordshire, Luton and Suffolk. We found a home to rent in Suffolk, searched many churches and found a New Frontier Church. I got a hospital transfer to the theatre wards of a Suffolk hospital and began working in caesarean sections and the delivery suites of the emergency theatres.

I had started a Psalm Drummer group and

it was running at about a steady thirty to forty people. Things were going really well. I felt called to serve the church in music and took up a position in the church as a worship leader, playing percussion one Sunday, drumming the next and leading the congregation with guitar and vocals too. Life had never been better. But the homosexuality problem was still playing on my mind.

There was a key group of Christians who knew, understood and supported me. I started to discuss the problem with Claire and we began to work with the pastors. We were praying and trusting that these feelings, that this life-long battle would go and never come back. I was married now with two children and I had made my choice to live in a heterosexual marriage. I was faithful but the struggle was immense.

One morning I woke up with flu-like symptoms and my chest felt very tight. I was struggling to breathe. I went to the doctor who thought I might be developing asthma, considering my family history. I was no better after being put on steroids. We returned to the doctor, who did a peak-flow measurement on me. He put me on an inhaler and a nebulizer which made no difference to my breathing. He admitted me to hospital straight away. I spent a very long time in hospital having chest x-rays and other tests. The conclusion was not asthma. They discharged me a few weeks later and they were awaiting the test results. My breathing didn't appear to be any better.

I was at home one day, shaving, and noticed in the mirror a tiny bump on my right ear. This mole-like thing kept growing and growing over the weeks. I went to the doctor again. He suspected it to be a Basel Cell Carcinoma, which was a benign tumour. It turned out to be a malignant melanoma. I had biopsies done and a course of treatment was needed. I spent many months in hospital and on morphine. I was off work for almost two years, battling skin cancer. And then one day it just left me. Praise God. The lessons I had learned about sickness and healing were to prove invaluable.

After the two-year battle with cancer was won, we decided to return home to my brother's house for Christmas dinner. It was the first Christmas dinner we'd had since my parents died some seventeen years earlier.

Some time later, Claire and I went back to Ireland for a holiday to visit family. During this visit there was a massive uproar in the town. There was high-profile publicity concerning clerical sexual abuse. A priest had overdosed in the wake of his trial for abusing young boys. The result was a non-statutory state inquiry into the abuse, the handling of abuse claims by the South Eastern Health Board, the Catholic Clergy and the An Garda Siochana. The inquiry became know as the 'Ferns Inquiry' as it centred on the Catholic Diocese of Ferns.

There was an organisation called 'One-in-four' set up by one of this priest's victims. When we returned to the UK after the holiday, I could not get it out of my head. They were asking members of the public to assist the inquiry and to come forward in confidence with their stories. I called them and told them my story over the phone. They suggested I come to the office and share with them the story. I did just that and before long I was called to the Ferns Inquiry, to share with them my story. In the build-up to the inquiry, I was offered counselling and they put me in touch with a counsellor in my area. I attended counselling every week and as the sessions unfolded, I managed to work through the issues of the abuse and the real source of the homosexuality. The guilt and the release were phenomenal. I progressed more in those two years of counselling, while the enquiry was going on, than I ever had in my entire life.

We reversed the lies that Denis Byrne had told me – the lies I adopted and believed. I learned valuable, life-changing lessons and my wife supported me through it all.

I was praying for release, that the damage done would be undone and that I would be free from the struggle. I returned home again, like I had done many times, to assist the inquiry by answering the questions concerning the abuse.

I met a man in Main Street in Gorey who happened to be Niamh's Dad. I asked him how Niamh was as I hadn't see her since I bumped into her in London by total accident in 1998. He told me that she had died of liver disease. Her marriage of three years had broken up and she had left London and returned home to die. My mouth dropped open. I was devastated. In nearly seventeen years I had cried only two, maybe three times. I went home to the UK and felt totally deflated and crushed. It hit me hard. At 1am I got into bed with Claire after getting in from the airport. I wept. It was five days later before my tears dried up. The release, the hurt, the pain were immeasurable. My friend, my soul mate – the one person who helped me through life in the early stages – the one who saved me from suicide and despair, the one woman who taught me how to make love to a woman – the one woman who sowed a seed in me that I was not gay, had died, and I wasn't there for her.

I returned to St Michael's cemetery and visited her grave. I could see St Michael's Church in the background, and I saw the shed that I had been abused in had been torn down. Was the Catholic Church destroying evidence? I thought: I have given my evidence to the Ferns Inquiry. I have told Claire everything about myself. I have come through so much in life. I could almost hear Niamh's voice calling from the grave. "Tell the story. Tell our story." I cried for hours, kneeling on her grave.

I returned to my wife in the UK. I decided, along with many other victims, that our story must come out. People must know, and understand. They must not be naïve when it comes to child abuse. People must find hope in our stories, and realise that this is a story the Catholic Church would pay millions to silence. I returned home and started writing.

Then the real pain and release came. The realisation came that, in order for this story to be true and real, I must actually practise forgiveness. This book could not be about hate, anger or vengeance. But I must respond to the challenges set out in the Bible. I must not be hypocritical. I must choose what was right. I was to start releasing forgiveness. God dealt with Denis Byrne, turned around the court, restored friendship and marriage following my lies. In the same way, he set me free to live the life he called me to live. He was going to show me how to forgive but at the same time I was to be a lion who would roar at injustice. I first had to forgive. It was not a popular idea.

Chapter 19

Forgiving Ferns

*"If we practise an eye for an eye and a tooth
for a tooth, soon the whole world will be blind and
toothless."*
Mahatma Gandhi

*"For if you forgive people their trespasses [their
reckless and wilful sins, leaving them, letting them go,
and giving up resentment], your heavenly Father will
also forgive you."*
Matthew 6:14

After appearing before the Ferns Inquiry team
and after numerous visits to the solicitors' office
in Dublin, I watched as the Diocese of Ferns
was brought to its knees. *The Birmingham Report,* later to be known as the *Ferns Report,* was
published on Tuesday 25th October 2005.

The report of the Ferns Inquiry says that it
identified more than 100 allegations of child
sexual abuse, made between 1962 and 2002,
against 21 priests.

Father Michael McCarthy acknowledged
along with Sergeant Doherty that they recalled
me making my allegations to the Diocese and

the An Garda.

Sergeant Doherty, now retired, acknowledged that he recalled taking the statements and remembers filing them in the Garda Report. A Garda investigation was underway as to why these reports were overlooked.

Father Michael McCarthy could not explain to the Ferns Inquiry team why he did not place me in counselling, why he failed to report the matter to the Diocese of Shrewsbury, why he failed to report the matter to the police, why he never condemned what happened to me, and why he never called what happened to me a crime.

The Ferns Inquiry could not continue to report on these important findings and has left it to a civil investigation and lawsuit to unearth the truth. The Terms of Reference of the Ferns Inquiry were to investigate abuse carried out by clergy. Father Denis Byrne was a seminarian at the time of the abuse, therefore did not fall under the terms of reference.

In my view, he was responsible to the Bishop of Ferns, Doctor Comiskey. He applied to him to become a student in the first place. He was ordained and served in the Diocese of Ferns as a priest. The Ferns Inquiry lawyers argued this but Judge Frank Murphy overruled and pushed the Inquiry to a close. We had no choice but to leave the case in the hands of civil lawyers and they are continuing in that regard.

Six of the priests died before any allegations of abuse were made against them.

The 271-page report by Justice Frank Murphy was presented to the Cabinet and was world news in a matter of weeks.

Dublin followed suit and set up its own independent inquiry and the Dublin Diocese abuse inquiry is set to be even greater than that of the Ferns Inquiry.

I have included, in the appendix at the back of this book, excerpts from the inquiry report about my case. In these extracts I am known as 'Brian'.

I can now say that, with the help of Jesus, I have forgiven Denis Byrne and I have forgiven the mistakes and deliberate errors of Father Matthew McCarthy and Sergeant Doherty.

I have never received an apology from the Catholic Church and my letters requesting to meet with them were ignored. But I will have justice. I will be acknowledged. I will not be gagged or silenced. I will tell the truth. Forgiveness does not mean we have to allow ourselves to be abused again. We forgive the past but we don't repeat the past.

As difficult as it seems, you can be sure of this – at the core of my heart, I have the power to move beyond the old issues that are still hindering my freedom. The hardest things – the ones that push me right up against my limits – are the very things I need to address to make a quantum leap into a fresh inner life.

Ultimately, it's not a question of whether they deserve to be forgiven. I am not forgiving them for their sake or because they have apologised, because they have yet to apologise.

I am forgiving them for myself, for my own health and well-being. Forgiveness is simply the most energy-efficient option.

It frees me from the incredibly toxic resentment, which can lead to cancer, depression, drug addiction and ultimately suicide. Holding a grudge is debilitating and draining.

Don't let these people live rent-free in your head. If they hurt you before, why let them keep doing it year after year in your mind? It's not worth it. But it takes God, your heart and real effort to stop it. You can muster that heart-power to forgive them as a way of looking out for yourself. It's one thing you can be totally selfish about.

I am taking it slowly. Forgiveness does not come overnight. I need to let it go step by step. The deepest resentments are wrapped up in a lot of hurt and pain. People think they're protecting themselves by not forgiving. But they are harming themselves.

As I acknowledge my wrong-doing – the terror I put my robbery victims through and the pains I put my wife through – it is that which allows me to go easy on myself and gradually release forgiveness to those who hurt me.

Forgiveness means that you've decided not to let it keep festering inside, even if it comes up once in a while. Forgiveness is a powerful yet challenging tool that will support and honour you, even in the most extreme circumstances.

The incoherence that results from holding on to resentments and unforgiving attitudes keeps you from being aligned with your true self. It can block you from your next level of quality life experience. Metaphorically, it's the curtain standing between the room you're living in now and a new room, much larger and full of beautiful objects.

The act of forgiveness removes the curtain. Clearing up your old accounts can free up so much energy that you jump right into a whole new house. Forgiving releases you from the punishment of a self-made prison, where you are both the inmate and the jailer.

Sincere forgiveness isn't coloured with expectations that the other person will apologise or change. Don't worry whether or not they finally understand you. Love them and release them. Life feeds back truth to people in its own way and its own time – just like it does for you and me.

Countless people are afraid to forgive because they feel they must remember the wrong or they will not learn from it. The opposite is true. Through forgiveness, the wrong is released from its emotional stranglehold on us so that we can learn from it. Through the power and intelligence of the heart, the release of forgiveness brings expanded intelligence to work with the situation more effectively.

It's been said that, "We give up leisure in order that we may have leisure, just as we go to war in order that we may have peace."
Aristotle, (384 - 322 BC)

I found these statements in the Bible as I have worked through my forgiveness:

"Wash me thoroughly [and repeatedly] from my iniquity and guilt and cleanse me and make

me wholly pure from my sin."

(Psalm 51:2)

"Create in me a clean heart, O God, and renew a right, persevering, and steadfast spirit within me. Cast me not away from your presence and take not your Holy Spirit from me. Restore to me the joy of your salvation and uphold me with a willing spirit."

(Psalm 51:10-12)

"He who covers and forgives an offence seeks love, but he who repeats or harps on a matter separates even close friends."

(Proverbs 17:9)

"If my people, who are called by my name, shall humble themselves, pray, seek, crave, and require of necessity my face and turn from their wicked ways, then will I hear from heaven, forgive their sin, and heal their land."

(2 Chronicles 7:14)

For me, the greatest example of forgiveness is Jesus Christ. Beaten with the Roman whip – with its razor tips – stripped naked and nailed to a cross of slow execution —was this not abuse? Yet as they hammered in the nails, he prayed for their forgiveness.

To forgive is to set a prisoner free and discover the prisoner was you.

The honest truth is that I will never forget what happened to me. All along the Church has sought a gagging order, so my story would be kept hidden. But that amounts to more abuse, a hiding of the truth in darkness and secrecy. I was silenced when I was 12 years old but I will not be silenced now. The world will know that writing this book is bringing me release and bringing the reader release and a challenge.

"If we [freely] admit that we have sinned and confess our sins, he is faithful and just (true to his own nature and promises) and will forgive our sins [dismiss our lawlessness] and [continuously] cleanse us from all unrighteousness [everything not in conformity to his will in purpose, thought, and action]."

(1 John 1:9)

Coming to this place at the cross of Jesus, you can realise what it is to be forgiven and in your own life you, too, can be released from your own 'Ferns'. The Diocese of Ferns, for me, was a place of darkness and fear – a living hell. I was a little boy and it seemed all the adults in positions of authority were more intent on covering up the abuse than protecting the victims. As you read this story you will see the bizarre twists and turns I have come through. I still have some work to do but you can see how it is possible, though difficult, for me to be arriving at a place where I am forgiving Ferns.

If we want to get free from our past, I believe we must begin by connecting with our Creator. I'll close with a prayer that millions of people around the world have used to begin their journey with God. If you want to come into a new life of peace, say this prayer and see what God does with your life.

Lord Jesus,

Please forgive me for the past.

I believe you died on the cross for me.

Today I give my life to you.

Please come into my life and into my heart.

Wash me clean on the inside.

Fill me with your Holy Spirit

and set me free.

And I will follow you all the days of my

life.

Amen.

APPENDIX

Excerpts about my case from the Ferns Inquiry report, in which I am referred to as 'Brian'.

p.106-107

4.12.1   BRIAN

Brian alleged the following:

Brian stated that whilst he was a 12-year-old altar boy in Wexford in 1984, Fr Byrne, then a final-year seminarian from St Peter's, attended his church for training. He abused Brian over a ten-month period on a weekly basis. The abuse began with fondling and touching but developed into oral sex and rape. Fr Byrne warned Brian against speaking to anyone about the abuse and sought to reassure Brian during these incidents that this behaviour was normal and regularly occurred at St Peter's College. Brian has told the Inquiry that the abuse had a very serious impact upon his life. For many years he believed he must have been homosexual to have caused a priest to behave in that way. It was not until his late 20s that he realised his sexual orientation was heterosexual and he formed a relationship with a woman to whom is now married. He believes that the trauma caused by the abuse still has repercussions for him. He also became involved in a life of crime for a short period and believes the abuse was responsible for that.

This seminarian was not ordained for the Diocese of Ferns but the fact that he was a seminarian in St Peter's College and served as a priest in the diocese for a short period between ordination and his appointment to a parish in England is, in the view of the Inquiry, significant.

Brian told Fr Matthew McCarthy about the abuse in detail but no action was taken by Fr McCarthy in spite of an assurance from him that he would inform the diocese. Fr McCarthy told this Inquiry that he remembers hearing a vague report from Brian but confused the alleged perpetrator with someone else and did not report it onwards. Brian also wrote to Bishop Comiskey and telephoned his offices on two occasions in respect of his complaint but did not receive a reply. No record of these contacts appears on diocesan files furnished to the Inquiry.

p.183

The Inquiry has recently been notified of a complaint made by Brian (4.12.1) which included allegations of serious sexual assault and rape by this priest in 1984 whilst he was still a seminarian in his final year in St Peter's College and on secondment to assist a church in the diocese. The abuse which occurred when Brian was 12 years of age continued for eight months. He was warned by Fr Byrne not to speak about it to anyone and did not do so until 1993 when he attended a series of meetings with Fr Matthew McCarthy.

According to Brian, Fr McCarthy wrote a detailed note of the allegation and undertook to pass it on to the Bishop of Ferns. Fr McCarthy has told the Inquiry that he remembers meeting Brian but believed that the allegations of child sexual abuse related to a lay worker in the church who had been charged with sexual offences. He did not therefore pass on the complaint although he indicated to Brian that he had done so.

Brian telephoned the bishop's secretary on a number of occasions and was assured that his desire for a meeting with the bishop would be passed on to him. The bishop never contacted Brian.

Fr Byrne was subsequently ordained for the diocese of Shrewsbury and is now deceased. It has been reported to the Inquiry that Fr McCa-

rthy told this complainant that he had forward-
ed his complaints to Bishop Comiskey. It is also
reported that the complaint was made to Bishop
Comiskey on three occasions in or about March
1993. It is further claimed that he reported these
complaints to two members of An Garda Sìo-
chàna. No evidence of his complaint appears on
Diocesan or Garda files.

Fr Byrne, although subsequently ordained
for another diocese, was operating in the Diocese of Ferns for some months after ordination
and the complaint against him was made to the
diocese and dealt with by church personnel in
the diocese.

CHAPTER 7 EXCERPT
FR DENIS BYRNE

The Inquiry was notified of a complaint by
Brian (4.14.1) against this former priest whilst
a seminarian at St Peter's College. The Inquiry
ascertained from speaking with a former sergeant at Gorey Station that a complaint of sexual abuse against this priest was made known
to him during the course of his interview with
Brian for various crimes in the area in or about
1993. The Inquiry was told by the complainant
that a separate statement was made to the Garda

in respect of such abuse. The former sergeant believed that details in respect of this complaint would have been recorded in the course of that interview and contained on the file relating to the complainant's criminal proceedings but no investigation took place in respect of Fr Byrne.

The Inquiry's view of the handling of complaints made against Fr Denis Byrne:

• The Inquiry is surprised that this complaint did not prompt an investigation of any kind into the serious and important matters to which the complaint related.

• The Inquiry is concerned that it has not been furnished with any Garda documents relating to this complaint.

available from
www.psalmdrummers.org

HEAVEN'S KING ALBUM

Released in November 2008 on the Kingsway Label

This is the latest collection of worship songs from Noel Richards, who currently has 17 songs in the CCLI Top 500 Church Copyright listing.

Recorded in Nashville, USA, produced by John Hartley, and featuring songs that Noel has co-written with Tricia Richards, Tom Lane, Kees Kraayenoord, Wayne Drain, Dave Clifton and Tim Sherrington.

Available from Christian Bookstores and online at

www.noelrichards.com

www.worshipjournal.com